Retirement Done Right

A Comprehensive Financial Guide

Todd Elliott | Elliott Financial Group

Copyright © 2020 by Todd Elliott.

All rights reserved. No part of this publication may be reproduced, distributed, or transmitted in any form or by any means, including photocopying, recording, or other electronic or mechanical methods, without the prior written permission of the publisher, except in the case of brief quotations embodied in critical reviews and certain other noncommercial uses permitted by copyright law. For permission requests, write to the publisher at the address below. These materials are provided to you by Todd Elliott for informational purposes only and Todd Elliott and Advisors Excel, LLC expressly disclaim any and all liability arising out of or relating to your use of same. The provision of these materials does not constitute legal or investment advice and does not establish an attorney-client relationship between you and Todd Elliott. No tax advice is contained in these materials. You are solely responsible for ensuring the accuracy and completeness of all materials as well as the compliance, validity, and enforceability of all materials under any applicable law. The advice and strategies found within may not be suitable for every situation. You are expressly advised to consult with a qualified attorney or other professional in making any such determination and to determine your legal or financial needs. No warranty of any kind, implied, expressed, or statutory, including but not limited to the warranties of title and non-infringement of third-party rights, is given with respect to this publication.

Todd Elliott / Elliott Financial Group
18001 N. 79th Ave., Suite A15
Glendale, AZ 85308
https://elliottfg.com/

Book layout ©2020 Advisors Excel, LLC

Retirement—Done Right Todd Elliott. 1st ed

ISBN 979-8-5854247-3-1

Todd Elliott is registered as an Investment Advisor Representative and is a licensed insurance agent. Elliott Financial Group is an independent financial services firm that helps individuals create retirement strategies using a variety of investment and insurance products to custom suit their needs and objectives.

The contents of this book are provided for informational purposes only and are not intended to serve as the basis for any financial decisions. Any tax, legal, or estate planning information is general in nature. It should not be construed as legal or tax advice. Always consult an attorney or tax professional regarding the applicability of this information to your unique situation.

Information presented is believed to be factual and up-to-date, but we do not guarantee its accuracy, and it should not be regarded as a complete analysis of the subjects discussed. All expressions of opinion are those of the author as of the date of publication and are subject to change. Content should not be construed as personalized investment advice nor should it be interpreted as an offer to buy or sell any securities mentioned. A financial advisor should be consulted before implementing any of the strategies presented.

Investing involves risk, including the potential loss of principal. No investment strategy can guarantee a profit or protect against loss in periods of declining values. Any references to protection benefits or guaranteed/lifetime income streams refer only to fixed insurance products, not securities or investment products. Insurance and annuity product guarantees are backed by the financial strength and claims-paying ability of the issuing insurance company.

Insight Folios Inc and Elliott Financial Group, Inc. are not affiliated companies.

Any names used in the examples in this book are hypothetical only and do not represent actual clients.

*To all of our clients, past, present and future . . .
Thank you!!!*

*You are not a true success
unless you are helping others be successful
~ Jon Gordon*

Table of Contents

The Importance of Planning i
Longevity 5
Taxes 21
Market Volatility 27
Retirement Income 35
Social Security 51
401(k)s & IRAs 67
Annuities 77
Estate & Legacy 85
Women-Specific Concerns 93
Finding a Financial Professional 105
Acknowledgments 109
About the Author 111

FOREWORD
The Importance of Planning

Would you trust a pilot who didn't have a plan? It takes tremendous concentration, experience, and effort to make a sixty-five-ton vehicle fly safely from point A to B. While you're eating your pretzels and sipping your soda, the pilot is directing the aircraft on a pre-planned flight course. He's prepared for potential challenges; he makes constant adjustments based on changing weather, air traffic, and other factors.

If the pilot had no plan, the aircraft would never leave the ground. If the pilot had a poor plan, the aircraft would never reach the ground without disaster. For the pilot, a good plan is the difference between life and death.

Planning for retirement isn't exactly the same as flying an airplane, but some would argue the stakes are almost as high. Sure, it doesn't mean life or death. But many retirees have confessed they'd rather die than outlive their money. With a bad plan, you could find yourself losing hundreds of thousands of vital income dollars. Conversely, a good plan can facilitate financial security and invaluable peace of mind.

Even with a good plan, you'll still have some concerns, and you're still going to have to make adjustments from time to time. But you'll be able to navigate to your retirement safely.

Planning for retirement, like planning to safely pilot a plane, takes effort, concentration, and experience. If you retire correctly, though, you're only going to do it once. So, how are you supposed to acquire prior experience?

Your Future

Do you feel prepared for the future? Whether you've been planning your retirement for decades, a few years, or less than a year, you've probably asked yourself at some point, "Will I be ready?"

Throughout our lives, we're bombarded with gratuitous advice. People tell us where to live, where to work, what to wear, what to eat . . . The list goes on and on. It's annoying. But, frankly, for as much unsolicited advice as we discard, there is often sound counsel to be had. Developing experience often means learning the hard way. Learning, while relying on the experience of others, has its advantages. No human is an expert in everything; to be successful, we must sometimes rely on the advice and direction of people we trust.

So, whose advice will you listen to? You must choose carefully. You're only as good as the advice you choose to follow.

When it comes to planning for retirement, where will you turn for sound advice?

Advice for Retirement

As a financial advisor, my goal for every client is the same. No matter who you are—whether you're a millionaire or just above the poverty line—you have the same needs, the same desires, and the same fundamental objective for retirement: you want to live comfortably with financial security.

I don't believe in handing off financial statements to a brokerage firm and letting them do what they think is best. I try to involve my clients. When clients are immersed in the planning process, they take ownership of it. It's not just some plan, it's *their* plan. Taking this approach also helps my clients to have more flexibility and to have a better outlook on their retirement.

Almost every financial advisor has that same big-picture mission. We all want to help you acquire and preserve assets you'll benefit from in the future. But, in finding the right advisor for you, you'll find the differences are in the details.

If you're looking for a financial advisor, you must find someone trustworthy. That's easier said than done. Forming and building trust is no simple matter. That's why good advisors make it their job to prove they have your best interests at heart.

Unfortunately, there are some advisors who just want to sell you something. They exert minimal effort to help clients or to build relationships. They're the thorns and thistles of the financial world. You must sift out such individuals.

Look for someone who doesn't work with just everybody. Rather, find an advisor who is as discerning in the decision to take you on as you are in selecting him or her. Advisors like that understand the commitment involved in assuming responsibility for someone's assets—they won't take it lightly. The right advisor understands your goals and is there when you have a question or want to talk. Once you find an advisor you trust, the best planning can begin.

When I help people to plan responsibly for their retirement, I see the happiness and confidence that comes from this preparation. Having a good plan for retirement won't allay every anxiety about the future, but it will give you a peace of mind that is truly invaluable.

As you read this book, you'll get a better idea of what is involved in planning for retirement. Don't let the next 120 pages intimidate you. Much of the retirement planning process involves basic principles. Some of it is more complicated, but don't worry—I'll step you through the process. This book is meant to get your wheels turning and your feet moving towards a plan that will benefit you in the many years to come. So, let's get started!

CHAPTER 1

Longevity

You would think the prospect of the grave would loom more frightening as we age, yet many retirees say their number one fear is actually running out of money in their twilight years.[1] This fear is, unfortunately, justified, in part, because of one significant factor: We're living longer.

According to the Social Security Administration, in 1950, the average life expectancy for a sixty-five-year-old man was seventy-eight, and the average for a sixty-five-year-old woman was eighty-one. In 2020, those averages were eighty-three and eighty-eight, respectively.[2]

The bottom line of many retirees' budget woes comes down to this: They just didn't plan to live so long. Now, when we are younger and in our working years, that's not something we necessarily see as a bad thing; don't some people fantasize about living forever or, at least, reaching the ripe old age of one hundred?

However, with a longer lifespan, as we near retirement, we face a few snags. Our resources are finite—we only have so much money to provide income—but our lifespans can be

---

[1] Samiha Khanna. Journal of Accountancy. February 14, 2019. "Clients' Top Fear: Running out of Money."
https://www.journalofaccountancy.com/news/2019/feb/top-retirement-fears-201920387.html
[2] Social Security Administration. 2011 Trustees Report. "Actuarial Publications: Cohort Life Expectancy."
https://www.ssa.gov/OACT/TR/2011/lr5a4.html

unpredictably long, perhaps longer than our resources allow. Also, longer lives don't necessarily equate with healthier lives. The longer you live, the more money you will likely need to spend on health care, even excluding long-term care needs like nursing homes.

You will also run into inflation. If you don't plan to live another twenty-five years but end up doing so, inflation at an average 2.5 percent will raise your $50,000-per-year budgeted need up to $93,000 per year. Or, if you live another eight years as inflation rises, you will need about $810,000 to cover those same expenses.[3] And this is before you count the expenses of any potential health care or long-term care needs.

Because we don't necessarily get to have our cake and eat it, too, our collective increased longevity hasn't necessarily increased the healthy years of our lives. Typically, our life-extending care most widely applies to the time in our lives where we will need more care in general. Think of common situations like a pacemaker at eighty-five, or cancer treatment at seventy-eight.

"Wow, Todd," I can hear you say. "Way to start with the good news first."

I know, I've painted a grim picture. But all I'm concerned about here is the cost. It's hard to put a dollar sign on life, but that is essentially what we're talking about when discussing longevity and your finances. According to the Stanford Center on Longevity, more than half of pre-retirees underestimate the life expectancy of the average sixty-five-year-old.[4] Living longer isn't a bad thing; it just costs more, and one key to a sound retirement strategy is preparing in advance for that expense.

---

[3] Katie Brockman. The Motley Fool. August 19, 2018. "More Americans are Living into Their 90s—and That's Bad News for Their Savings."
https://www.fool.com/retirement/2018/08/19/more-americans-are-living-into-their-90s-and-thats.aspx

[4] Stanford Center on Longevity. "Underestimating Years in Retirement."
http://longevity.stanford.edu/underestimating-years-in-retirement/

A man once came into my office and asked to do some planning. I hadn't worked with him before, so I started going through a list of his assets. He had obviously done a fair amount of planning before coming to me. The more we talked, the more impressed I was by how well he had done. I asked him, "How old are you? Seventy-nine? Eighty? No more than eighty-one, right?"

He said, "I like you! I'm ninety-nine and I'll be one hundred in August." I was beside myself. The fact he had preserved his assets so well, and for so long, was outstanding. But, he was still planning and making adjustments to do better. That was even *more* remarkable.

This is a guy who did it right. He planned well, factoring in his longevity. His funds lasted him through multiple recessions, depressions, ups and downs in the market, all the way through a hundred years of life.

A good plan can work wonders.

Retiring Later

Planning for a long life in retirement partly depends on when you retire. While many people end up retiring earlier than they anticipated—due to injuries, layoffs, family crises, and other unforeseen circumstances—continuing to work past age sixty (and even sixty-five) is still a viable option for others and can be an excellent way to help establish financial comfort in retirement.

There are many reasons for this. For one, you obviously still earn a paycheck and the benefits accompanying it. Medical coverage and beefing up your retirement accounts with further savings can be significant by themselves but continuing your income also should keep you from dipping into your retirement funds, further allowing them the opportunity to grow.

Additionally, for many workers, their nine-to-five job is more than just clocking in and out. Having a sense of purpose can keep us active physically, mentally, and socially. That kind of activity and level of engagement may also help stave off many of the health problems that plague retirees. Avoiding a sedentary life is one of the advantages of staying plugged into the workforce, if possible.

A client of mine retired at age fifty-nine after a career as an engineer. He started golfing every day and traveling regularly. After a while, he told me he was bored out of his skull. He wanted to do something that would allow him to be around more people. So, he started working as a greeter at a department store. He had a seven-figure portfolio—obviously he didn't need the money. But, this work gave him a satisfaction his previous retirement hadn't.

Now, for those who do need the money, could you transition to a job that's less stressful but still provides income? You could kill two birds with one stone. This solution would preserve your retirement income and provide work that gives you a sense of purpose.

Health Care

Take a second to reflect on your health care plan. Although working up to or even past age sixty-five would allow you to avoid a coverage gap between your working years and Medicare, that may not be an option for you. Even if it is, when you retire, you will need to make some decisions about what kind of insurance coverage you may need to supplement your Medicare. Are there any medical needs you have that may require coverage in addition to Medicare? Did your parents or grandparents have any inherited medical conditions you might consider using a special savings plan to cover?

These are all questions that are important to review with your financial professional so you can be sure you have enough money put aside for health care.

Long-Term Care

Longevity means the need for long-term care is statistically more likely to happen. If you intend to pass on a legacy, planning for long-term care is paramount, since most estimates project nearly 70 percent of Americans will need some type of it.[5] However, this may be one of the biggest, most stressful pieces of longevity planning I encounter in my work. For one thing, who wants to talk about the point in their lives when they may feel the most limited? Who wants to dwell on what will happen if they no longer can toilet, bathe, dress, or feed themselves?

I get it; this is a less-than-fun part of planning. But a little bit of preparation now can go a long way!

When it comes to your longevity, just like with your goals, one of the important things to do is sit and dream. It may not be the fun, road-trip-to-the-Grand-Canyon kind of dreaming, but you can spend time envisioning how you want your twilight years to look.

For instance, if it is important for you to live in your home for as long as possible, who will provide for the day-to-day fixes and to-dos of housework if you become ill? Will you set aside money for a service, or do you have relatives or friends nearby whom you could comfortably allow to help you? Do you prefer in-home care over a nursing home or assisted living? This could be a good time to discuss the possibility of moving into a retirement community versus staying where you are or whether it's worth moving to another state and leaving relatives behind.

These are all important factors to discuss with your spouse and children, as *now* is the right time to address questions and concerns. For instance, is aging in place more important to one spouse than the other? Are the friends or relatives who live

---

[5] Moll Law Group. 2019. "The Cost of Long-Term Care." https://www.molllawgroup.com/the-cost-of-long-term-care.html

nearby emotionally, physically, and financially capable of helping you for a time if you face an illness?

Many families I meet with find these conversations very uncomfortable, particularly when children discuss nursing home care with their parents. A knee-jerk reaction for many is to promise they will care for their aging parents. This is noble and well-intentioned, but there needs to be an element of realism here. Does "help" from an adult child mean they stop by and help you with laundry, cooking, home maintenance, and bills? Or does it mean they move you into their spare room when you have hip surgery? Are they prepared to help you use the restroom and bathe if that becomes difficult for you to do on your own?

I don't mean to discourage families from caring for their own; this can be a profoundly admirable relationship when it works out. However, I've seen families put off planning for late-in-life care based on a tenuous promise that the adult children would care for their parents, only to watch as the support system crumbles. Sometimes this is because the assumed caregiver hasn't given serious thought to the preparation they would need, both in a formal sense and regarding their personal physical, emotional, and financial commitments. This is often also because we can't see the future: Alzheimer's disease and other maladies of old age can exact a heavy toll. When a loved one reaches the point where he or she is at risk of wandering away or needs help with two or more activities of daily living, it can be more than one person or family can realistically handle.

If you know what you want, communicate with your family about both the best-case and worst-case scenarios. Then, hope for the best, and plan for the worst.

Realistic Cost of Care

Wrapped up in your planning should be a consideration for the cost of long-term care. Although many of us will need some degree of long-term care—including the 30 percent of us who may need up to five years of facility care—60 percent of us underestimate the costs of nursing home care. On average, consumers underestimate the annual cost of a private room in a nursing home by 51 percent.[6]

Another piece of planning for long-term care costs is anticipating inflation. It's common knowledge prices have been, and keep, rising, and that will lower your purchasing power on everything from food to medical care. Long-term care is a big piece of the inflation-disparity pie, which is part of why many find their estimates of nursing home care widely miss the mark. According to one survey, people expected to pay around $25,350 in out-of-pocket long-term care expenses per year, but, in reality, they'll more likely be paying over $47,000.[7]

While local costs vary from state to state, here's the national median for various forms of long-term care (plus projections that account for a 3 percent annual inflation, so you can see what I'm talking about):[8]

---

[6] Tamara E. Holmes. Yahoo Finance. July 24, 2019. "Consumers Underestimate Costs of Long-Term Care." https://finance.yahoo.com/news/consumers-underestimate-costs-long-term-173542918.html

[7] Moll Law Group. 2019. "The Cost of Long-Term Care." https://www.molllawgroup.com/the-cost-of-long-term-care.html

[8] Genworth Financial. June 2018. "Cost of Care Survey 2018." https://www.genworth.com/aging-and-you/finances/cost-of-care.html

Long-Term Care Costs: Inflation				
	Home Health Care, Homemaker Services	Adult Day Care	Assisted Living	Nursing Home (semi-private room)
Annual 2019	$51,480	$19,500	$48,612	$90,155
Annual 2029	$69,185	$26,206	$65,330	$121,161
Annual 2039	$92,979	$35,219	$87,799	$162,830
Annual 2049	$124,955	$47,332	$117,994	$218,830

Fund Your Long-Term Care

One critical mistake I see are those who haven't planned for long-term care because they assume the government will provide everything. But that's a big misconception. The government has two health insurance programs: Medicare and Medicaid. These can greatly assist you in your health care needs in retirement but usually don't provide enough coverage to cover all your health care costs in retirement. My firm isn't a government outpost, so we don't get to make decisions when it comes to forming policy and specifics about either one of these programs. I'm going to give the overview of both, but if you want to dive into the details of these programs, you can visit www.Medicare.gov and www.Medicaid.gov.

Medicare

Medicare covers those aged sixty-five and older and those who are disabled. Medicare's coverage of any nursing-home-related health issues is limited. It might cover your nursing home stay if it is not a "custodial" stay, and it isn't long-term. For example, if you break a bone or suffer a stroke, stay in a nursing home for rehabilitative care, and then return home, Medicare may cover you. But, if you have developed dementia or are looking to move to a nursing facility because you can no longer bathe, dress, toilet, feed yourself, or take care of your hygiene, etc., then Medicare is not going to pay for your nursing home costs.[9]

Medicaid

Medicaid is a program the states administer, so funding, protocol, and limitations vary. Compared to Medicare, Medicaid more widely covers nursing home care, but it targets a different demographic than Medicare: those with low incomes.

If you have more assets than the Medicaid limit in your state and need nursing home care, you will need to use those assets to pay for your care. You will also have a list of additional state-approved ways to spend some of these assets over the Medicaid limit, such as pre-purchasing burial plots and funeral expenses or paying off debts. After that, your remaining assets fund your nursing home stay until they are gone, at which point Medicaid will jump in.

Some people aren't stymied by this, thinking they will just pass on their financial assets early, gifting them to relatives, friends, and causes so they can qualify for Medicaid when they need it. However, to prevent this exact scenario, Uncle Sam has implemented the look-back period. Currently, if you enroll in Medicaid, you are subject to having the government scrutinize

---

[9] Medicare.gov. "What Part A covers." https://www.medicare.gov/what-medicare-covers/part-a/what-part-a-covers.html

the last five years of your finances for large gifts or expenses that may subject you to penalties, temporarily making you ineligible for Medicaid coverage.

So, if you're planning to preserve your money for future generations and retain control of your financial resources during your lifetime, you'll probably want to prepare for the costs of longevity beyond a "government plan."

Self-Funding

One way to fund a longer life is the old-fashioned way, through self-funding. There are a variety of financial tools you can use, and they all have their pros and cons. If your assets are in low-interest financial vehicles (savings, bonds, CDs), you risk letting inflation erode the value of your dollar. Or, if you are relying on the stock market, you have more growth potential, but you'll also want to consider the possible implications of market volatility. What if your assets take a hit? If you suffer a loss in your retirement portfolio in early or mid-retirement, you might have the option to "tighten your belt," so to speak, and cut back on discretionary spending to allow your portfolio the room to bounce back. But, if you are retired and depend on income from a stock account that just hit a downward stride, what are you going to do?

HSAs

These days, you might also be able to self-fund through a health savings account, or HSA, if you have access to one through a high-deductible health plan (you will not qualify to save in an HSA after enrolling in Medicare). In an HSA, any growth of your tax-deductible contributions will be tax-free, and any distributions paid out for qualified health costs are also tax-free. Long-term care expenses count as health costs, so, if this is an option available to you, it is one way to use the tax advantages to self-fund your longevity. Bear in mind, if you are younger than sixty-five, any money you use for nonqualified expenses will be subject to taxes and penalties, and, if you are older than sixty-five, any HSA money you use for non-medical expenses is subject to income tax.

LTCI

One slightly more nuanced way to pay for longevity, specifically for long-term care, is long-term care insurance, or LTCI. As car insurance protects your assets in case of a car accident and home insurance protects your assets in case something happens to your house, long-term care insurance aims to protect your assets in case you need long-term care in an at-home or nursing home situation.

As with other types of insurance, you will pay a monthly or annual premium in exchange for an insurance company paying for long-term care down the road. Typically, policies cover two to three years of care, which is adequate for an "average" situation: it's estimated 70 percent of Americans will need about three years of long-term care of some kind. However, it's important to consider you might not be "average" when you are preparing for long-term care costs; on average, 20 percent of today's sixty-five-year-olds could need care for longer than five years.[10]

Now, there are a few oft-cited components of LTCI that make it unattractive for some:
- Expense — LTCI can be expensive. It is generally less expensive the younger you are, but a fifty-five-year-old couple who purchased LTCI in 2019 could expect to pay $3,050 each year for an average three-year coverage

---

[10] David Levine. *U.S. News*. July 10, 2019. "How to Pay for Nursing home Costs." https://health.usnews.com/best-nursing-homes/articles/how-to-pay-for-nursing-home-costs

policy. And the annual cost only increases from there the older you are.[11]

- Limited options — Let's face it: LTCI may be expensive for consumers, but it can also be expensive for companies that offer it. With fewer companies willing to take on that expense, this narrows the market, meaning opportunities to price shop for policies with different options or custom benefits are limited.
- If you know you need it, you might not be able to get it — Insurance companies offering LTCI are taking on a risk that you may need LTCI. That risk is the foundation of the product—you may or may not need it. If you know you will need it because you have a dementia diagnosis or another illness for which you will need long-term care, you will likely not qualify for LTCI coverage.
- Use it or lose it—If you have LTCI and are in the minority of Americans who die having never needed long-term care, all the money you paid into your LTCI policy is gone.
- Possibly fluctuating rates—Your rate is not locked in on LTCI. Companies maintain the ability to raise or lower your premium amounts. This means some seniors face an ultimatum: Keep funding a policy at what might be a less affordable rate *or* lose coverage and let go of all the money they paid in so far.

After that, you might be thinking, "How can people possibly be interested in LTCI?" But let me repeat myself—as many as 70 percent of Americans will need long-term care. And, although only 8 percent of Americans have purchased LTCI, keep in mind the high cost of nursing home care. Can you afford $7,000 a month to put into nursing home care and still have

---

[11] American Association for Long-Term Care Insurance. January 2019. "2019 National Long-Term Care Insurance Price Index." https://www.aaltci.org/news/wp-content/uploads/2019/01/2019-Price-Index-LTC.pdf

enough left over to protect your legacy? This is a very real concern: One study says 72 percent of Americans are impoverished by the end of just one year in a nursing home.[12] So, not to sound like a broken record, but it is vitally important to have a plan in place to deal with longevity and long-term care if you intend to leave a financial legacy.

I am licensed to sell long-term care insurance, but I'm judicious in recommending it. I've seen both the risks and benefits of these insurance products. The statistics on the need for long-term care make the benefits obvious. At the same time, there is a lot of variability and variety in available LTCI products. When choosing a long-term care insurance policy, you must carefully consider your circumstances and the terms of the policy. How a particular product functions might not suit your needs or cover you in certain situations. Some people assume their family will house them and care for them in their final years of life. But, when that time comes, health conditions and other factors can make that hope an impossibility. Other people plan extensively for long-term care but never end up needing it.

The bottom line: Be realistic and do your research.

Product Riders

LTCI and self-funding are not the only ways to plan for the expenses of longevity. Some companies are getting creative with their products, particularly insurance companies. One way they are retooling to meet people's needs is through optional product riders on annuities and life insurance. Elsewhere in this book, I talk about annuity basics, but here's a brief overview: Annuities are insurance contracts. You pay the insurance company a premium, either as a lump sum or as a series of payments over a set amount of time, in exchange for

---

[12] A Place for Mom. January 2018. "Long-Term Care Insurance: Costs & Benefits." http://www.aplaceformom.com/senior-care-resources/articles/long-term-care-costs

guaranteed income payments. One of the advantages of an annuity is it has access to riders, which allow you to tweak your contract for a fee, usually about 1 percent of the contract value annually. One annuity rider some companies offer is a long-term care rider. If you have an annuity with a long-term care rider and are not in need of long-term care, your contract behaves as any annuity contract would—nothing changes. Generally speaking, if you reach a point when you can't perform multiple functions of daily life on your own, you notify the insurance company, and a representative will turn on those provisions of your contract.

Like LTCI, different companies and products offer different options. Some annuity long-term care riders offer coverage of two years in a nursing home situation. Others cap expenses at two times the original annuity's value. It greatly depends. Some people prefer this option because there isn't a "use-it-or-lose-it" piece; if you die without ever having needed long-term care, you still will have had the income benefit from the base contract. Still, as with any annuities or insurance contracts, there are the usual restrictions and limitations. Withdrawing money from the contract will affect future income payments, early distributions can result in a penalty, income taxes may apply, and, because the insurance company's solvency is what guarantees your payments, it's important to do your research about the insurance company you are considering purchasing a contract from.

Understandably, a discussion on long-term care is bound to feel at least a little tedious. Yet, this is a critical piece of planning for income in retirement, particularly if you want to leave a legacy.

Failing to consider the need for long-term care can be detrimental.

One couple whom I advised wanted to purchase an LTCI policy. They were up in age but had impeccable health. As we were discussing policies and filling out the paperwork to apply, the wife was diagnosed with pre-dementia. This disqualified them from purchasing LTCI. Within a year, she was declared incompetent, and, a year after, her husband had to put her in a long-term care facility. She was there for another two years before she passed away. Because her condition required special care, the monthly expenses incurred from her stay were substantial.

Don't postpone a decision on long-term care.

Spousal Planning

Here's one thing to keep in mind no matter how you plan to save: Many of us will be planning for more than ourselves. Look back at all the stats on health events and the likelihood of long life and long-term care. If they hold true for a single individual, then the likelihood of having a costly health or long-term care event is even higher for a married couple. You'll be planning for not just one life, but two. So, when it comes to long-term care insurance, annuities, self-funding, or whatever strategy you are looking at using, be sure you are funding longevity for the both of you.

I remember a man I worked with who did it right. He and his wife purchased a LTCI policy when they were young. For about twenty years they went back and forth about dropping the policy. Ultimately, they kept it. After forty years of marriage, his wife had to be admitted to a long-term care facility. At first, expenses were at about $3,000 per month. But, as her health deteriorated, expenses climbed to well over $10,000 per month. She was in this facility for five years before passing away. Thankfully, their insurance policy covered a sizable amount of the expense. Imagine how things would have turned out had they canceled this policy.

Factoring in the longevity of both you and your spouse when assessing your future needs is critical. Plan carefully and be ready for anything.

CHAPTER 2

Taxes

Where to begin with taxes? Perhaps by acknowledging we all bear responsibility for the resources we share. Roads, bridges, schools . . . It is the patriotic duty of every American to pay their fair share of taxes. Many would agree with me, though, while they don't mind paying their fair share, they're not interested in paying one cent more than that!

Now, just talking taxes probably takes your mind to April—tax season. You are probably thinking about all the forms you collect and how you file. Perhaps you are thinking about your certified public accountant or another qualified tax professional and saying to yourself, "I've already got taxes taken care of, thanks!"

However, what I see when people come into my office is that their relationship with their tax professional is purely a January through April relationship. That means they may have a tax professional, but not a tax *planner*.

What I mean is tax planning extends beyond filing taxes. In April, we are required to settle our accounts with the IRS to make sure we have paid up on our bill or to even the score if we have overpaid. But real tax planning is about making each financial move in a way that allows you to keep the most money in your pocket and out of Uncle Sam's.

Now, as a caveat, I want to emphasize I am neither a CPA nor a tax planner, but I see the way taxes affect my clients, and I have plenty of experience helping clients implement tax-efficient strategies in their retirement plans in conjunction with their tax professionals.

There are many outstanding tax professionals out there, and I'm privileged to work with one. My partner firm knows the ins and outs of tax law. They are quick to save you a buck when you had no idea there was money to be saved. For this reason and others, I frequently consult with tax professionals.

That being said, each professional must stay within their lane of expertise. When constructing a building, you have different tradesman using their skills to create a structure that will last. Imagine if you had the electrician doing the plumbing and the plumber doing the framing. This could impede the building's progress, or worse, compromise the structure entirely.

The same is true in the financial world. We are building effective strategies to preserve and grow the assets of our clients. In order to do that, we must collaborate. When we put together the skills of a tax professional and a financial professional, we can create the best retirement plan for you.

It is especially important to me to help my clients develop tax-efficient strategies in their retirement plans because each dollar they can keep in their pockets is a dollar we can put to work.

There is a reason tax professionals exist. Our tax system is complex. So complex that entire careers are dedicated to helping people understand and navigate this system. It could be compared to sailing through a windy, rocky sea. If you don't know the waters, you can easily be taken off course or run aground. Without the right planning, you could be hit by tax rates that make your plans for retirement sink like a ship in a tumultuous sea.

Planning for taxes can save you tens of thousands of dollars. If that isn't motivation enough, think about the kind of vacation you could take if you had an extra ten grand in your pocket when you retire.

The Fed

Now, in the United States, taxes can be a rather uncertain proposition. Depending on who is in the White House and which party controls Congress, we might be tempted to assume tax rates could either decline or increase in the next four to eight years accordingly. However, there is one (large!) factor we, as a nation, must confront: the national debt.

Currently, according to USDebtClock.org, we are over $26,500,000,000,000 in debt and climbing. That's $26.5 *trillion* with a "T." With just $1 trillion, you could park it in the bank at a zero percent interest rate and still spend more than $54 million every day for fifty years without hitting a zero balance.

Even if Congress got a handle and stopped that debt from its daily compound, divided by each taxpayer, we each would owe about $214,000. So, will that be check or cash?

My point here isn't to give you anxiety. I'm just saying, even with the rosiest of outlooks on our personal income tax rates, none of us should count on low tax rates for the long term. Instead, you and your network of professionals (tax, legal, and financial) should constantly be looking for ways to take advantage of tax-saving opportunities as they come. After all, the best "luck" is when proper planning meets opportunity.

So, How Can We Get Started?: Know Your Limits

One of the foundational pieces of tax planning is knowing what tax bracket you are in, based on your income after subtracting pre-tax or untaxed assets. Your income taxes are based on your taxable income.

One reason to know your taxable income and your income tax rate is so you can see how far away you are from the next lower or higher tax bracket. This is particularly important when it comes to decisions such as gifting and Roth IRA rollovers.

For instance, based on the 2020 tax table, Mallory and Ralph's taxable income is just over $330,000, putting them in the 32 percent tax bracket and about $3,400 above the upper end of the 24 percent tax bracket. They have already maxed out their retirement funds' tax-exempt contributions for the year. Their daughter, Gloria, is a sophomore in college. This couple could shave a considerable amount off their tax bill if they use the $3,400 to help Gloria out with groceries and school—something they were likely to do, anyway, but now can deliberately be put to work for them in their overall financial strategy.

Now, I use Mallory and Ralph only as an example—your circumstances are probably different—but I think this nicely illustrates the way planning ahead for taxes can save you money.

Assuming a Lower Tax Rate

Many people anticipate being in a lower tax bracket in retirement. It makes sense: You won't be contributing to retirement funds; you'll be drawing from them. And you won't have all those work expenses—work clothes, transportation, etc.

Yet, do you really plan on changing your lifestyle after retirement? Do you plan to cut down on the number of times you eat out, scale back vacations, and skimp on travel?

What I see in my office is many couples spend more in the first few years, or maybe the first decade, of retirement. Sure, that may taper off later on, but usually only just in time for their budget to be hit with greater health and long-term care expenses. Do you see where this is going? Many people plan as though their taxable income will be lower in retirement and are surprised when the tax bills come in and look more or less the same as they used to. It's better to plan for the worst and hope for the best, wouldn't you agree?

401(k)/IRA

One sometimes-unexpected piece of tax planning in retirement concerns your 401(k) or IRA. Most of us have one of these accounts or an equivalent. Throughout our working lives, we pay in, dutifully socking away a portion of our earnings in these tax-deferred accounts. There's the rub: tax-deferred. Not tax-free. Very rarely is anything free of taxation when you get down to it. Using 401(k)s and IRAs in retirement is no different. The taxes the government deferred when you were in your working years are now coming due, and you will pay taxes on that income at whatever your current tax rate is.

Just to ensure Uncle Sam gets his due, the government also has a required minimum distribution, or RMD, rule. Beginning at age seventy-two, you are required to withdraw a certain minimum amount every year from your 401(k) or IRA, or else you will face a 50 percent tax penalty on any RMD monies you should have withdrawn but didn't—and that's on top of income tax.

Of course, there is also the Roth account. You can think of the difference between a Roth and a traditional retirement account as the difference between taxing the seed and taxing the harvest. Because Roths are funded with post-tax dollars, there aren't tax penalties for early withdrawals of the principal nor are there taxes on the growth after you reach age fifty-nine-and-one-half. Perhaps best of all, there are no RMDs. Of course, you must own a Roth account for a minimum of five years before you are able to take advantage of all its features.

This is one more area where it pays to be aware of your tax bracket. Some people may find it advantageous to "convert" their traditional retirement account funds to Roth account funds in a year during which they are in a lower tax bracket.

Others may opt to put any excess RMDs from their traditional retirement accounts into other products, like stocks or insurance.

Does that make your head spin? Understandable. That's why it's so important to work with a financial professional and tax planner who can help you not only execute these sorts of tax-efficient strategies but also help you understand what you are doing and why.

If you take nothing else from this chapter, remember: Developing effective tax strategies is crucial. I cannot emphasize that enough. This is especially true as our tax system changes, and as tax brackets, standard deductions, and viable write-offs are adjusted constantly.

If you need help to find a qualified tax professional, or you feel like you need a new one, my firm can help. We have a network of people we trust with tax-related issues. They can offer a fresh pair of eyes or a second opinion on your unique tax situation.

CHAPTER 3

Market Volatility

Up and down. Roller coaster. Merry-go-round. Bulls and bears. Peak-to-trough.

Sound familiar? This is the language we use to talk about the stock market. With volatility and spikes, even our language is jarring, bracing, and vivid.

Still, financial strategies tend to revolve around market-based products, for good reasons. For one thing, there is no other financial class that packs the same potential for growth, pound for pound, as stock-based products. Because of growth potential, inflation protection, and new opportunities, it may be unwise to avoid the market entirely.

However, along with the potential for growth is the potential for loss. Many of the people I see in my office come in still feeling a bit burned from the market drama of 2000 to 2010. That was a rough stretch, and many of us are once-bitten-twice-shy investors, right?

So how do we balance these factors? How do we try to satisfy both the need for protection and the need for growth?

For one thing, it is important to recognize the value of diversity. Now, I'm not just talking about the diversity of assets among different kinds of stocks, or even different kinds of stocks and bonds. That's only one kind of diversity; while important, both stocks and bonds, though different, are both still market-based products. Most market-based products, even within a diverse portfolio, tend to rise or lower as a whole, just like an incoming tide. Therefore, a portfolio diverse in only market-sourced products won't automatically protect your assets during times when the market declines.

In addition to the sort of "horizontal diversity" you have by purchasing a variety of stocks and bonds from different companies, I encourage having "vertical diversity," or diversity among asset classes. This means having different product types, including securities products, bank products, and insurance products—with varying levels of growth potential, liquidity, and protection—all in accordance with your unique situation, goals, and needs.

Market volatility isn't going away. Nothing is going to change its effect on our financial system. What we *can* change is how we prepare for it.

People with more money typically have a higher tolerance for bad investments in a volatile market. If they make a few bad moves, it's not going to affect their lives or their retirement. On the other hand, people with less money have a lower tolerance; bad investments can wreck their retirement plan. Still, no one wants to waste money. Everyone needs the same caution and the same principles to invest wisely.

There are products designed to remain stable when the market is bad. But they limit growth when the market is good. There are other products that maximize growth when the market is going that way. However, when the market tanks, all is lost. Finding the right balance between these products is all part of the art of financial planning.

If you plan right, you don't have to worry about if, when, and how much the market is going to change. You'll be ready for anything and everything.

The Color of Money

When you're looking at the overall diversity of your portfolio, part of the equation is knowing which products fit in what category: what has liquidity, what has protection, and what has growth potential.

Before we dive in, keep in mind these aren't absolutes. You might think of liquidity, growth, and protection as primary colors. While some products will look pretty much yellow, red, or blue, others will have a mix of characteristics, making them more green, orange, or purple.

Growth

I like to think of the growth category as red. It's powerful, it's somewhat volatile, and it's also the category where we have the greatest opportunities for growth and loss. Often, products in the growth category will have a good deal of liquidity but very little protection. These are our market-based products and strategies, and we think of them mostly in shades of red and orange, to designate their growth and liquidity. This is a good place to be when you're young—think fast cars and flashy leather jackets—but its allure often wanes as you move closer to retirement. Examples of "red" products include:

- Stocks
- Equities
- Exchange-traded funds
- Mutual funds
- Corporate bonds
- Real estate investment trusts
- Speculations
- Alternative investments

Liquidity

Yellow is my liquid category color. I typically recommend having at least enough yellow money to cover six months' to a year's worth of expenses in case of emergency. Yellow assets

don't need a lot of growth potential; they just need to be readily available when we need them. The "yellow" category includes:
- Cash
- Money market accounts

Protection

The color of protection, to me, is blue. Tranquil, peaceful, sure, even if it lacks a certain amount of flash. This is the direction I like to see people generally move toward as they're nearing retirement. The red, flashy look of stock market returns and the risk of possible overnight losses is less attractive as we near retirement and look for more consistency and reliability. While this category doesn't come with a lot of liquidity, the products here are backed by an insurance company, a bank, or a government entity. "Blue" products include:
- Certificates of deposit (backed by banks)
- Government-based bonds (backed by the U.S. government)
- Life insurance (backed by insurance companies)
- Annuities (backed by insurance companies)

While not specifically mentioned above, I'm a firm believer in dividends. Dividends fall into the growth and liquid category; you can think of them as orange in color.

A dividend is a payment given to a stockholder by a corporation. So, dividends are a form of income you receive from holding stock in a company. Not every stock you purchase will yield a dividend. After you receive one, the value of your stock may drop. But what you earn from dividends is yours. This passive source of income is one I seriously recommend to my clients. Creating a dividend portfolio can add a powerful boost to your retirement plan.

Carefully choosing the right products takes time. When balancing products in your portfolio, keep this in mind: Single digit returns are far better than double digit losses.

401(k)s

I want to take a second to specifically address a product many retirees will be using to build their retirement income: the 401(k) and other retirement accounts. Any of these retirement accounts (IRAs, 401(k)s, 403(b)s, etc.) are basically "tax wrappers." What do I mean by that? Well, depending on your plan provider, a 401(k) could include target-date funds, passively managed products, stocks, bonds, mutual funds, or even variable, fixed, and fixed index annuities, all collected in one place and governed by rules (a.k.a. the "tax wrapper"). These rules govern how much money you can put inside, what ways you can put it in, when you will pay taxes on it, and when you can take the money out. Inside the 401(k), each of the products inside the "tax wrapper" might have its own fees or commissions, in addition to the management fee you pay on the 401(k) itself.

Now, fees can be troublesome. You can't get something for nothing, and fees are how many financial companies and professionals make a living. Yet, it's important to recognize even a fee of a single percentage point is money out of your pocket—money that represents not just the one-time fee of today but also represents an opportunity cost. One study found a single percentage point fee could cost a millennial close to $600,000 over forty years of saving.[13] For someone closer to retirement, how much do you think fees may have cost?

---

[13] Dayana Yochim and Jonathan Todd. NerdWallet. "How a 1% Fee Could Cost Millennials $590,000 in Retirement Savings." https://www.nerdwallet.com/blog/investing/millennial-retirement-fees-one-percent-half-million-savings-impact/

Even for those close to retirement, it's important to look at management fees and assess if you think you're getting what you pay for. Over the course of ten years, those puppies can add up, and you may have decades ahead of you in which you will need to rely on your assets.

Dollar-Cost Averaging

With 401(k)s and other market-based retirement products, when you are investing for the long term, dollar-cost averaging is a concept that can work in your favor. When the market is trending up, if you are consistently paying in money, month over month, great; your investments can grow, and you are adding to your assets. When the market takes a dip, no problem; your dollars buy more shares at a lower price. At some point, we hope the market will rebound, in which case your shares can grow and possibly be more valuable than they were before. This concept is what we call dollar-cost averaging. While it can't ensure a profit or guarantee against losses, it's a time-tested strategy for investing in a volatile market.

However, when you are in retirement, this strategy may work against you. You may have heard of "reverse" dollar-cost averaging. Before, when the market lost ground, you were "bargain-shopping"; your dollars purchased more assets at a reduced price. When you are in retirement, you are no longer the purchaser; you are selling. So, in a down market, you have to sell more assets to make the same amount of money as what you made in a favorable market.

I've had lots of people step into my office to talk to me about this, emphasizing, "My advisor says the market always bounces back, and I have to just hold on for the long term."

There's some basis for this thinking; thus far, the market has always rebounded to higher heights than before. But this is no guarantee, and the prospect of potentially higher returns in five years may not be very helpful in retirement if you are relying on the income from those returns to pay this month's electric bill, for example.

Is There a "Perfect" Product?

To bring us back around to the discussion of protection, growth, and liquidity, the ideal product would be a "ten" in all three categories, right? Completely guaranteed, doubling in size every few years, and accessible whenever you want. Does such a product exist? Anyone who says "yes" is either ignorant or malevolent.

Instead of running in circles looking for that perfect product, the silver bullet, the unicorn of financial strategies, it's more important to circle back to the concept of a balanced, asset-diverse portfolio.

This is why your interests may be best served when you work with a trusted financial professional who knows what various financial products can do and how to use them in your personal retirement plan.

Also, remember inflation complicates matters. Inflation cripples the safest strategies because it corrodes your assets over time. Even if you wanted to save your money by stashing cash under your mattress, it would still be slowly undermined by inflation.

You need to balance a conservative strategy with one that promotes growth. Only then can you do what is truly safest for your assets. Inflation makes achieving balance more difficult, but it makes creating this balance critical to preserving your assets.

CHAPTER 4

Retirement Income

Retirement. For many of us, it's what we've saved for and dreamed of, pinning our hopes to a magical someday. Is that someday full of traveling? Is it filled with grandkids? Gardening? Maybe your fondest dream is simply never having to work again, never having to clock in or be accountable to someone else.

Your ability to do these things all hinges on *income*. Without the money to support these dreams, even a basic level of work-free lifestyle is unsustainable. That's why planning for your income in retirement is so foundational. But where do we begin?

It's easy to feel overwhelmed by this question. Some may feel the urge to amass a large lump sum and then try to put it all in one product—insurance, investments, liquid assets—to provide all the growth, liquidity, and income they need. Instead, I think you need a more balanced approach. After all, retirement planning isn't magic. Like I mention elsewhere, there is no single product that can be all things to all people (or even all things to one person). No approach works unilaterally for everyone. That's why it's important to talk to a financial professional who can help you lay down the basics and take you step-by-step through the planning process. Not only will you have the assurance that you have addressed the areas you need to, but you will also have an ally who can help you break down the process and help keep you from feeling overwhelmed.

Sources of Income

Thinking of all the pieces of your retirement expenses might be intimidating. But, like cleaning out a junk drawer or revisiting that garage remodel, once you have laid everything out, you can begin to sort things into categories.

Once you have a good overall picture of where your expenses will lie, you can start stacking up the resources to cover them.

Social Security

Social Security is a guaranteed, inflation-protected federal insurance program playing a significant part in most of our retirement plans. From delaying until you've reached full retirement age or beyond to examining spousal benefits, as I discuss elsewhere in this book, there is plenty you can do to try to make the most of this monthly benefit. As with all your retirement income sources, it's important to consider how to make this resource stretch to provide the most bang and buck for your situation.

Pension

Another generally reliable source of retirement income for you might be a pension, if you are one of the lucky people who still has one.

If you don't have a pension, go ahead and skim on to the next section. If you do have a pension, keep on reading.

Because your pension can be such a central piece of your retirement income plan, you will want to put some thought into answering basic questions about it.

How well is your pension funded? Since the heyday of the pension plan, companies and governments have neglected to fund their pension obligations, causing a persistent problem with this otherwise reliable asset. Public pensions face a collective $4.7 trillion deficit, according to the U.S. Pension Tracker.[14] The Public Benefit Guaranty Association, which helps insure private pensions, reports there is a $54 billion shortfall in multiemployer plans, affecting half of all multiemployer plans.[15] If you have a pension, it is quite possibly included in those statistics.

In addition to checking up on your pension's health, check into what your options are for withdrawing your pension. If you have already retired and made those decisions, this may be a foregone conclusion. If not, it pays to know what you can expect and what decisions you can make, such as taking spousal options to cover your husband or wife if he or she outlives you.

Also, some companies are incentivizing lump-sum payouts of pensions to reduce the companies' payment liabilities. If that's the case with your employer, talk to your financial professional to see if it might be prudent to do something like that or if it might be better to stick with lifetime payments or other options.

Your 401(k) and IRA

One "modern way" to save for retirement is in a 401(k) or IRA (or their nonprofit or governmental equivalents). These tax-advantaged accounts are, in my opinion, a poor substitute for pensions, but one of the biggest disservices we do to ourselves is to not take full advantage of them in the first place. According to one article, about 42 percent of adults under thirty and 26

---

[14] U.S. Pension Tracker. April 2019. us.pensiontracker.org
[15] Alessandro Malito. MarketWatch. December 11, 2018. "The Truth About Pensions: They Aren't Dead, But Some Are Barely Holding On." https://www.marketwatch.com/story/the-truth-about-pensions-they-arent-dead-but-some-are-barely-holding-on-2018-12-11

percent of adults thirty to forty-four haven't contributed to any retirement account, let alone their 401(k).[16]

Also, if you have changed jobs over the years, do the work of tracking down any benefits from your past employers. You might have an IRA here or a 401(k) there; keep track of those so you can pull them together and look at those assets when you're ready to look at establishing sources of retirement income.

Do You Have...

- Life insurance?
- Annuities?
- Long-term care insurance?
- Any passive income sources?
- Stock and bond portfolios?
- Liquid assets? (What's in your bank account?)
- Alternative investments?
- Rental properties?

It's important, if you are going through the work of sitting with a financial professional, to look at your full retirement income picture and pull together *all* your assets, no matter how big or small. From the free insurance policy offered at your bank to the sizable investment in your brother-in-law's modestly successful furniture store, you want to have a good idea of where your money is.

Some years ago, a husband and wife came to me to assess their financial situation. The husband had been retired for five years. The wife was considering retirement. She was pulling in

---

[16] Niall McCarthy. Forbes. June 3, 2019. "Report: A Quarter of Americans Have No Retirement Savings."
https://www.forbes.com/sites/niallmccarthy/2019/06/03/report-a-quarter-of-americans-have-no-retirement-savings-infographic/#5fb35b703ebf

over $100,000 a year, so their concern was whether they would have enough to offset this income. They also had a beautiful house in Paradise Valley, Arizona. They wanted to keep the home through their retirement. One advisor they consulted ran the numbers and said they came up short. When I gave their portfolio a fresh look, I assessed *all* their assets and calculated their expenses, and, as it turned out, they had more money than they realized. There were accounts they had forgotten about or didn't think were important enough to consider, but pulling it all into one plan made a significant difference. The wife retired that fall.

This couple planned well over the years and constantly kept a pulse on their situation. This allowed them to retire right when they wanted to.

Pulling together your assets to accurately assess how much you have is absolutely necessary to make good decisions for your retirement. You might have more than you expect.

Retirement Income Needs

How much income will you need in retirement? How do you determine that? A lot of people work toward a random number, thinking, "If I can just have a million dollars, I'll be comfortable in retirement!" Don't get me wrong; it is possible to save up a lot of money and then retire in the hopes you can keep your monthly expenses lower than some set estimation. But I think this carries a general risk of running out of money. Instead, I work with my clients to find out what their current and projected income needs are and then work from there to see how we might cover any gaps between what they have and what they want.

Goals and Dreams

I like to start with your pie in the sky. Do you find yourself planning for your vacations more thoroughly than you do your retirement? A recent survey found one in five Americans spends more time planning vacations than planning retirements.[17] Maybe it's because planning a vacation is less stressful: Having a week at the beach go awry is, well, a walk on the beach compared to running out of money in retirement. Whatever the case, perhaps it would be better if you thought of your retirement as a vacation in and of itself—no clocking in, no boss, no overtime. If you felt unlimited by financial strain, what would you do?

Would an endless vacation for you mean Paris and Rome? Would it mean mentoring at children's clubs or serving at the local soup kitchen? Or maybe it would mean deepening your ties to those immediately around you—neighbors, friends, and family. Maybe it would mean more time to take part in the hobbies and activities you love. Have you been considering a second (or even third) act as a small-business owner, turning a hobby or passion into a revenue source?

This is your time to daydream and answer the question: If you could do anything, what would you do?

After that, it's a matter of putting a dollar amount on it. What are the costs of round-the-world travel? One couple I know said their highest priority in retirement was being able to take each of their grandchildren on a cross-country vacation every year. That's a pretty specific goal—one that is reasonably easy to nail down a budget for.

I've seen many of my clients attain what they had always dreamed of during their retirement. They were able to achieve their goals and dreams because they factored them into a plan.

---

[17] Malika Mitra. CNBC. August 2, 2019. "You're not alone if you spend more time planning your vacation than working on your finances." https://www.cnbc.com/2019/08/02/1-in-5-people-spend-more-time-planning-vacations-than-finances-survey.html

Current Budget

Compiling a current expense report is one of the trickiest pieces of retirement preparation. Many people assume the expenses of their lives in retirement will be different—lower. After all, there will be no drive to work, no need for a formal wardrobe, and, perhaps most impactful of all, no more saving for retirement!

Yet, we often underestimate our daily spending habits. That's why I typically ask my clients to bring in their bank statements for the past year—they are reflective of your *actual* spending, not just what you think you're spending.

People have different lifestyles. Some live a simple lifestyle, while others are used to living with a lot more. As humans, we're creatures of habit. Thinking that you will live a simpler life in retirement, or, conversely, a more lavish life, isn't realistic. Your plan should reflect that your expenses aren't going to drop dramatically. Also, your income won't magically triple once you start withdrawing from your retirement accounts.

Remembering this will help you to assess your expenses properly and to understand your income.

The point: *Be Realistic.*

During this step of the process, you must look at the big picture. I always tell my clients that it's better to run out of life before running out of money.

I can't count the number of times I have sat with a couple, asked them about their spending, and heard them throw out a number that seemed incredibly low. When I ask them where the number came from, they usually say they estimated based on their total bills. Yet, our spending is so much more than our mortgage, utilities, cable, phone, car, grocery, or credit card bills.

"What about clothes?" I ask, "Or dining out? What about gifts and coffees and last-minute birthday cards?" That's when the lights come on.

This is why I suggest collecting a year's worth of information. There is usually no such thing as a one-time purchase. Did you buy new furniture? Even if that is a rarity, do you think that will be the last time you *ever* buy furniture?

Another hefty expense is spending on the kids. Many of the couples I work with are quick to help their adult children, whether it's something like letting them live in the basement, paying for college, babysitting, paying an occasional bill, or contributing to a grandchild's college fund. They aren't alone—79 percent of Americans in 2018 said they had provided financial support for an adult child. And it's not unlikely for some parents to tap into their retirement funds to do so.[18]

My clients sometimes protest that what they do for their grown children can stop in retirement. They don't *need* to help. But I get it. Parents like to feel needed. And, while you never want to neglect saving for retirement in favor of taking on financial risks (like your child's student debt), the parents who help their adult children do so, in part, because it helps them feel fulfilled.

When it comes down to expenses, including (and especially) spending on your family, don't make your initial calculations based on what you *could* whittle your budget down to if you *had* to. Instead, start from where you are. Who wants to live off a bare-bones bank account in retirement?

Other Expenses

Once you have nailed down your current budget and your dreams or goals for retirement, there are a few other outstanding pieces to think about—some expenses many people don't take the time to consider before making and

---

[18] Lorie Konish. CNBC. October 2, 2018. "Parents Spend Twice as Much on Adult Children than They Save for Retirement."
https://www.cnbc.com/2018/10/02/parents-spend-twice-as-much-on-adult-children-than-saving-for-retirement.html

executing a plan. But, I'm assuming you're different and want to get it right, so let's take a look.

Housing

Do you know where you want to live in retirement? This makes up a substantial piece of your income puzzle—since the typical American household owns a home, and it's generally their largest asset—but it often goes unaccounted for until the last minute. [19]

Some people prefer to live right where they are for as long as they can. Others have been waiting for retirement to pull the trigger on an ambitious move, like purchasing a new house, or even downsizing. Whatever your plans and whatever your reasons, there are quite a few things to consider.

Mortgage

Do you still have a mortgage? What may have been a nice tax boon in your working years could turn into a financial burden in your retirement. After all, when you are on a limited income, a mortgage is just one more bill sapping your financial strength. It is something to put some thought into, whether you plan to age in place or are considering moving to your dream home, buying a house out of state, or living in a retirement community.

Upkeep and Taxes

A house without a mortgage still requires annual taxes. While it's tempting to think of this as a once-a-year expense, when you

---

[19] Jann Swanson. Mortgage News Daily. August 28, 2019. "Homeownership is the Top Contributor to Household Wealth." http://www.mortgagenewsdaily.com/08282019_homeownership.asp

have limited earning potential, your annual tax bill might be something into which you should put a little more forethought.

The costs of homeownership aren't just monetary. When you find yourself dealing with more house than you need, it can drain your time and energy. From keeping clutter at bay to keeping the lawn mower running, upkeep can be extensive and expensive. For some, that's a challenge they heartily accept and can comfortably take on. For others, the idea of yard work or cleaning an area larger than they need feels foolish.

For instance, Peggy discovered after her knee replacement that most of her house was inaccessible to her when she was laid up.

"It felt ridiculous to pay someone else to dust and vacuum a house I was only living in 40 percent of!"

Practicality and Adaptability

Erik and Magda are looking to retire within the next two decades. They just sold their old three-bedroom ranch-style house. Their twins are in high school, and the couple has wanted to "upgrade" for years. Now they live in a gorgeous 1940s three-story house with all the kitchen space they ever wanted, five sprawling bedrooms, and a library and media room for themselves and their children. Within months of moving in, the couple realized a house perfect for their active teens would no longer be perfect for them in five to fifteen years.

"We are paying the mortgage for this house, but we've started saving for the next one," said Magda, "because who wants to climb two flights of stairs to their bedroom when they're seventy-eight?"

Others I know have encountered a similar situation in their personal lives. After a health crisis, one couple found the luxurious tub for two they toiled to install had become a specter of a bad slip and a potential safety risk. It's important to think through what your physical reality could be. I always emphasize to my clients that they should plan for whatever their long-term future might hold, but it's amazing how many people don't give it much thought.

Contracts and Regulations

If you are looking into a cross-country move, be aware of new tax tables or local ordinances in the area where you are looking to move. After all, you don't want to experience sticker-shock when you are looking at downsizing or reducing your bills in retirement.

Along the same lines, if you are moving into a retirement community, be sure to look at the fine print. What happens if you must move into a different situation for long-term care? Will you be penalized? Will you be responsible for replacing your slot in the community? What are all the fees, and what do they cover?

Inflation

As I write this in 2020, America has experienced a long stretch of low inflation, with inflation not exceeding 4 percent since 1991.[20]

However, inflation isn't a one-time bump; it has a cumulative effect. Even with relatively low inflation over the past few decades, the $20 sneakers you bought your grade-schooler in 1991 will cost $37.90 to buy for your grandchild today.[21] What if, in retirement, we hit a stretch like the late '70s and early '80s, when annual inflation rates of 10 percent became the norm? It may be wise to consider some extra

---

[20] US Inflation Calculator. January 2020. "Historical Inflation Rates." http://www.usinflationcalculator.com/inflation/historical-inflation-rates/
[21] Ibid.

padding in your retirement income plan to account for any potential increase in inflation in the future.

Aging

Also, in the expense category, think about longevity. We all hope to age gracefully. However, it's important to face the prospect of aging with a sense of realism.

The elephant in the room for many families is long-term care: No one wants to admit they will likely need it, but estimates say as many as 70 percent of us will.[22] Aging is a significant piece of retirement income planning because you'll want to figure out how to set aside money for your care, either at home or away from it. The more comfortable you get with discussing your wishes and plans with your loved ones, the easier planning for the financial side of it can be.

I discuss health care and potential long-term care costs in more detail elsewhere in this book, but, suffice it to say, nursing home care tends to be very expensive and typically isn't something you get to choose when you will need.

It isn't just the costs of long-term care that pose a concern in living longer. It's also about covering the possible costs of everything else associated with living longer. For instance, if Henry retires from his job as a biochemical engineer at age sixty-five, perhaps he planned to have a very decent income for twenty years, until age eighty-five. But what if he lives until he's ninety-five? That's a whole third—ten years—more of personal income he will need.

---

[22] Moll Law Group. 2019. "The Cost of Long-Term Care." https://www.molllawgroup.com/the-cost-of-long-term-care.html.

Putting It All Together

Whew! So, you have pulled together what you have, and you have a pretty good idea of where you want to be. Now your financial professional and you can go about the work of arranging what assets you *have* to cover what you *need*—and how you might try to cover any gaps.

Like the proverbial man in the Bible who built his house on a rock, I like to help my clients figure out how to cover their day-to-day living expenses—their needs—with insurance and other guaranteed income sources like pensions and Social Security.

Start from the ground up. That's my policy when assessing whether a client is ready to retire. When you carefully calculate everything—all your expenses, all your income, and everything in between—it becomes clear where you stand. Being this thorough might seem like a chore, but it will give you confidence in your retirement future.

Again, you should keep in mind there isn't one single financial vehicle, asset, or source to fill all your needs, and that's okay. One of the challenges of planning for your income in retirement concerns figuring out what products and strategies to use. You can release some of that stress when you accept the fact you will probably need a diverse portfolio—potentially with bonds, stocks, insurance, and other income sources—not just one massive money pile.

One way to help shore up your income gaps is by working with your financial professional and a qualified tax advisor to mitigate your tax exposure. If you have a 401(k) or IRA, a tax advisor in your corner can help you figure out how and when to take distributions from your account in a way that doesn't push you into a higher tax bracket. Or you might learn how to use tax-advantaged bonds more effectively. Effective tax planning isn't necessarily about "adding" to your income. Especially regarding retirement, it's less about what you make than it is about what you keep. Paying a lower tax bill keeps more money in your pocket, which is where you want it when it comes to retirement income.

Now you can look at ways to cover your remaining retirement goals. Are there products like long-term care insurance specific to a certain kind of expense you anticipate? Is there a particular asset you want to use for your "play" money—money for trips and gifts for the grandkids? Is there any way you can portion off money for those charitable legacy plans?

Once you have analyzed your income wants, needs, and the assets to realistically cover them, you may have a gap. The masterstroke of a competent financial professional will be to help you figure out how you will cover that gap. Will you need to cut out a round of golf a week? Maybe skip the new car? Or will you need to take more substantial action?

One way to cover an income gap is to consider working longer or even part-time before retirement and even after that magical calendar date. This may not be the best "plan" for you; disabilities, work demands, and physical or emotional limitations can hinder the best-laid plans to continue working. However, if it is physically possible for you, this is one considerable way to help your assets last, for more than one reason.

In fact, about one in five Americans are still working past age sixty-five. This is a record percentage in the past half-century. While some do list their personal finances as a reason for staying on the job, others do so to avoid feeling bored in retirement, among other reasons.[23]

That being said, many people have the desire to retire outright. If that is your desire, we can meet it with the right amount of planning.

Many of my clients are surprised at how soon they can retire. I've seen blue-collar workers, who expected to be working in

---

[23] Associated Press. October 9, 2018. "1 in 5 Americans over 65 are Still Waiting to Retire." https://nypost.com/2018/10/09/1-in-5-americans-over-65-are-still-waiting-to-retire/

their trade until their eighties, find they have enough to retire much earlier.

Running the numbers and carefully counting the costs is the key. At first glance, calculating your retirement income could appear overwhelming. But, as you've seen through this chapter, it can be done. Giving this aspect of your retirement plenty of forethought will help you be ready for anything.

When you're retired, you no longer have an employer paying you a steady check. It is up to you to make sure you have saved and planned for the income you need.

CHAPTER 5

Social Security

Social Security is often the foundation of retirement income. Backed by the strength of the U.S. Treasury, it provides perhaps the most dependable paycheck you will have in retirement.

From the time you collect your first paycheck from the job that made you a bonafide taxpayer, you pay into the grand old Social Security system. (For me, I was a dishwasher at a restaurant in Missoula, Montana, when I was sixteen years old.) What grew and developed out of the pressures of the Great Depression has become one of the most popular government programs in the country, and if you pay in for the equivalent of ten years or more, you, too, can benefit from the Social Security program.

Now, before we get into the nitty-gritty of Social Security, I'd like to address a current concern: Will Social Security still be there for you when you reach retirement age?

The Future of Social Security

This question is ever-present as headlines trumpet an underfunded Social Security program, alongside the sea of baby boomers who are retiring in droves and the comparatively smaller pool of younger people who are bearing the responsibility of funding the system.

The Social Security Administration itself acknowledges this concern as each Social Security statement now bears an asterisk that continues near the end of the summary:

> "*Your estimated benefits are based on current law. Congress has made changes to the law in the past and can do so at any time. The law governing benefit amounts may change because, by 2034, the payroll taxes collected will be enough to pay only about 79 percent of scheduled benefits."

Just a reminder, as if you needed one, that nothing in life is guaranteed. Additionally, depending on who you're listening to, Social Security funds may run low before 2034, thanks to the financial instability and government spending that accompanied the 2020 COVID-19 pandemic.

Before you get too discouraged, though, here are a few thoughts to keep you going:

- Even if the program is only paying 79 cents on the dollar for scheduled benefits, 79 percent is notably not zero.
- The Social Security Administration has made changes in the distant and near past to protect the fund's solvency, including increasing retirement ages and striking certain filing strategies.
- There are many changes Congress could make, and lawmakers are currently discussing how to fix the system, such as further increasing full retirement age and eligibility.
- One thing no one is seriously discussing? Reneging on current obligations to retirees or the soon-to-retire.

Take heart. The real answer to the question, "Will Social Security be there for me?" is still "yes."

This question is an important one to consider when you look at how much we, as a nation, rely on this program. Did you know Social Security benefits replace about 40 percent of a person's original income when they retire?[24]

If you ask me, that's a pretty significant piece of your retirement income puzzle.

Another caveat? You may not realize this, but no one can legally "advise" you about your Social Security benefits.

"But, Todd," you may be thinking, "isn't that part of what you do? And what about that nice gentleman at the Social Security Administration office I spoke with on the phone?"

Don't get me wrong. Social Security Administration employees know their stuff. They are trained to know policies and programs, and they are usually pretty quick to tell you what you can and cannot do. But the government specifically says, because Social Security is a benefit you alone have paid into and earned, your Social Security decisions, too, are yours alone.

When it comes to financial professionals, we can't push you in any directions, either, *but*—there's a big but here—working with a well-informed financial professional is still incredibly handy when it comes to your Social Security decisions. Why? Because someone who's worth his or her salt will know what withdrawal strategies might pertain to your specific situation and will ask questions that can help you determine what you are looking for when it comes to your Social Security.

For instance, some people want the highest possible monthly benefit. Others want to start their benefits early, not always because of financial need. I heard about one man who called in to start his Social Security payments the day he qualified, just because he liked to think of it as the government paying back a debt it owed him, and he enjoyed the feeling of receiving a check from Uncle Sam.

Whatever your reasons, questions, or feelings regarding Social Security, the decision is yours alone; but working with a financial professional can help you put your options in perspective by showing you—both with industry knowledge and

---

[24] Social Security Administration. "Learn About Social Security Programs." https://www.ssa.gov/planners/retire/r&m6.html

with proprietary software or planning processes—where your benefits fit into your overall strategy for retirement income.

One reason the federal government doesn't allow for "advice" related to Social Security, I suspect, is so no one can profit from giving you advice related to your Social Security benefit—or from providing any clarifications. Again, this is a sign of a good financial professional. Those who are passionate about their work will be knowledgeable about what benefit strategies might be to your advantage and will happily share those possible options with you.

Full Retirement Age

When it comes to Social Security, it seems like many people only think so far as "yes." They don't take the time to understand the various options available. Instead, because it is common knowledge you can begin your benefits at age sixty-two, that's what many of us do. While more people are opting to delay taking benefits, age sixty-two is still firmly the most popular age to start.[25]

What many people fail to understand is, by starting benefits early, they may be leaving a lot of money on the table. You see, the Social Security Administration bases your monthly benefit on two factors: your earnings history and your full retirement age (FRA).

From your earnings history, they pull the thirty-five years you made the most money and use a mathematical indexing formula to figure out a monthly average from those years. If you paid into the system for less than thirty-five years, then every year you didn't pay in will be counted as a zero.

---

[25] Elizabeth O'Brien. Money. March 7, 2019. "This is the Age when Most People Claim Social Security—and When Experts Say You Really Should." http://money.com/money/5637694/this-is-the-age-when-most-people-claim-social-security-and-when-experts-say-you-really-should/

Once they have calculated what your monthly earning would be at FRA, the government then calculates what to put on your check based on how close you are to FRA. FRA was originally set at sixty-five, but, as the population aged and lifespans lengthened, the government shifted FRA later and later, based on an individual's year of birth. Check out the following chart to see when you will reach FRA.[26]

---

[26] Social Security Administration. "Full Retirement Age." https://www.ssa.gov/planners/retire/retirechart.html

Age to Receive Full Social Security Benefits*

(Called "full retirement age" [FRA] or "normal retirement age.")

Year of Birth*	FRA
1937 or earlier	65
1938	65 and 2 months
1939	65 and 4 months
1940	65 and 6 months
1941	65 and 8 months
1942	65 and 10 months
1943-1954	66
1955	66 and 2 months
1956	66 and 4 months
1957	66 and 6 months
1958	66 and 8 months
1959	66 and 10 months
1960 and later	67

*If you were born on Jan. 1 of any year, you should refer to the previous year. (If you were born on the 1st of the month, we figure your benefit [and your full retirement age] as if your birthday was in the previous month.)

When you reach FRA, you are eligible to receive 100 percent of whatever the Social Security Administration says is your full monthly benefit.

Starting at age sixty-two, for every year before FRA you claim benefits, your monthly check is reduced by 5 percent or more. Conversely, for every year you delay taking benefits past FRA, your monthly benefit increases by 8 percent (until age seventy—after that, there is no monetary advantage to delaying Social Security benefits). While your circumstances and needs may vary, a lot of financial professionals still urge people to at least consider delaying until they reach age seventy.

Why Wait?[27]

Taking benefits early could affect your monthly check by _____.								
62	63	64	65	FRA 66	67	68	69	70
-25%	-20%	-13.3%	-6.7%	0	+8%	+16%	+24%	+32%

My Social Security

If you are over age thirty, you have probably received a notice from the Social Security Administration telling you to activate something called "My Social Security." This is a handy way to learn more about your particular benefit options, to keep track of what your earnings record looks like, and to calculate the benefits you have accrued over the years.

Essentially, My Social Security is an online account you can activate to see what your personal Social Security picture looks like, which you can do at www.ssa.gov/myaccount. This can be

---

[27] Social Security Administration. April 2019. "Can You Take Your Benefits Before Full Retirement Age?"
https://www.ssa.gov/planners/retire/applying2.html

extremely helpful when it comes to planning for income in retirement and figuring up the difference between your anticipated income versus anticipated expenses.

My Social Security is also helpful because it's a great way to see if there is a problem. For instance, I have heard of one woman who, through diligently checking her tax records against her Social Security profile, discovered her Social Security check was shortchanging her, based on her earnings history. After taking the discrepancy to the Social Security Administration, they sent her what they owed her in makeup benefits.

COLA

Social Security is a largely guaranteed piece of the retirement puzzle: If you get a statement that says to expect $1,000 a month, you can be sure you will receive $1,000 a month. But there is one variable detail, and that is something called the cost-of-living adjustment, or COLA.

The COLA is an increase in your monthly check meant to address inflation in everyday life. After all, your expenses will likely continue to experience inflation in retirement, but you will no longer have the opportunity for raises, bonuses, or promotions you had when you were working. Instead, Social Security receives an annual cost-of-living increase tied to the Department of Labor's Consumer Price Index for Urban Wage Earners and Clerical Workers, or CPI-W. If the CPI-W measurement shows inflation rose a certain amount for regular goods and services, then Social Security recipients will see that reflected in their COLA.

The COLA averages 4 percent, but in a no- or low-inflation environment, such as in 2010, 2011, and 2016, Social Security recipients will not receive an adjustment. Some view the COLA as a perk, bump, or bonus, but, in reality, it works more like this: Your mom sends you to the store with $2.50 for a gallon of milk. Milk costs exactly $2.50. The next week, you go back with that same amount, but it is now $2.52 for a gallon, so you go back to Mom, and she gives you 2 cents. You aren't bringing home more milk—it just costs more money.

So the COLA is less about "making more money" and more about keeping seniors' purchasing power from eroding when inflation is a big factor, such as in 1975, when it was 8 percent![28] Still, don't let that detract from your enthusiasm about COLAs; after all, what if Mom's solution was: "Here's the same $2.50; try to find pennies from somewhere else to get that milk!"?

Spousal Benefits

We've talked about FRA, but another big Social Security decision involves spousal benefits.

If you or your spouse has a long stretch of zeros in your earnings history—perhaps if one of you stayed home for years, caring for children or sick relatives—you may want to consider filing for spousal benefits instead of filing on your own earnings history. A spousal benefit can be up to 50 percent of the primary wage earner's benefit at full retirement age.

To begin drawing a spousal benefit, you must be at least sixty-two years old, and the primary wage earner must have already filed for his or her benefit. While there are penalties for taking spousal benefits early (you could lose up to 67.5 percent of your check for filing at age sixty-two), you cannot earn credits for delaying past full retirement age. [29]

Like I said, the spousal benefit can be a big deal for those who don't have a very long pay history, but it's important to weigh your own earned benefits against the option of withdrawing based on a fraction of your spouse's benefits.

---

[28] Social Security Administration. "Cost-Of-Living Adjustment (COLA) Information for 2019." https://www.ssa.gov/cola/.

[29] Social Security Administration. "Retirement Planner: Benefits For You As A Spouse." https://www.ssa.gov/planners/retire/applying6.html

To look at how this could play out, let's use a hypothetical example of Mary Jane, who is sixty, and Peter, who is sixty-two.

Let's say Peter's benefit at FRA, in his case sixty-six, would be $1,600. If Peter begins his benefits right now, four years before FRA, his monthly check will be $1,200. If Mary Jane begins taking spousal benefits in two years at the earliest date possible, her monthly benefits will be reduced by 67.5 percent, to $520 per month (remember, at FRA, the most she can qualify for is half of Peter's FRA benefit).

What if Peter and Mary Jane both wait until FRA? At sixty-six, Peter begins taking his full benefit of $1,600 a month. Two years later, when she reaches age sixty-six, Mary Jane will qualify for $800 a month. By waiting until FRA, the couple's monthly benefit goes from $1,720 to $2,400.

What if Peter delays until age seventy to get his maximum possible benefit? For each year past FRA he delays, his monthly benefits increase by 8 percent. This means, at seventy, he could file for a monthly benefit of $2,112. However, delayed retirement credits do not affect spousal benefits, so as soon as Peter files at seventy, Mary Jane would also file (at age sixty-eight) for her maximum benefit of $800, so their highest possible combined monthly check is $2,912.[30]

When it comes to your Social Security benefits, you obviously will want to consider whether a monthly check based on a fraction of your spouse's earnings will be comparable to or larger than your own earnings history.

Divorced Spouses

There are a few considerations for those of us who have gone through a divorce. If you 1) were married for ten years or more *and* 2) have since been divorced for at least two years *and* 3)

---

[30] Office of the Chief Actuary. Social Security Administration. "Social Security Benefits: Benefits for Spouses." https://www.ssa.gov/OACT/quickcalc/spouse.html#calculator

are unmarried *and* 4) your ex-spouse qualifies to begin Social Security, you qualify for a spousal benefit based on your ex-husband or ex-wife's earnings history at FRA. A divorced spousal benefit is different from the married spousal benefit in one way: You don't have to wait for your ex-spouse to file before you can file yourself.[31]

For instance, Charles and Moira were married for fifteen years before their divorce, when he was thirty-six and she was forty. Moira has been remarried for twenty years, and, although Charles briefly remarried, his second marriage ended after a few years. Charles' benefits are largely calculated based on his many years of volunteering in schools, meaning his personal monthly benefit is close to zero.

Although Moira has deferred her retirement, opting to delay benefits until she is seventy, Charles can begin taking benefits calculated from Moira's work history at FRA as early as sixty-two. However, he will also have the option of waiting until FRA to collect the maximum, or 50 percent of Moira's earned monthly benefit at her FRA.

Widowed Spouses

If your marriage ended with the death of your spouse, you might claim a benefit for your spouse's earned income as his or her widow/widower, called a "survivor's benefit." Unlike a spousal benefit or divorced benefits, if your husband or wife dies, you can claim his or her full benefit. Also, unlike spousal benefits, if you need to, you can begin taking income when you turn sixty. However, as with other benefit options, your monthly check will be permanently reduced for withdrawing benefits before FRA.

---

[31] Social Security Administration. "Retirement Planner: If You Are Divorced." https://www.ssa.gov/planners/retire/divspouse.html

If your spouse began taking benefits before he or she died, you can't delay withdrawing your survivor's benefits to get delayed credits; the Social Security Administration says you can only get as much from a survivor's benefit as your deceased spouse might have gotten, had he or she lived.[32]

Taxes, Taxes, Taxes

With Social Security, as with everything, it is important to consider taxes. It may be surprising, but your Social Security benefits are not tax-free. Despite having been taxed to accrue those benefits in the first place, you may have to pay Uncle Sam income taxes on up to 85 percent of your Social Security.

The Social Security Administration figures these taxes using what they call "the provisional income formula." Your provisional income formula differs from the adjusted gross income you use for your regular income taxes. Instead, to find out how much of your Social Security benefit is taxable, the Social Security Administration calculates it this way:

Provisional Income = Adjusted Gross Income + Nontaxable Interest + ½ of Social Security

See that piece about nontaxable interest? That generally means interest from government bonds and notes. It surprises many people that, although you may not pay taxes on those assets, their income will count against you when it comes to Social Security taxation.

---

[32] Social Security Administration. "Social Security Benefit Amounts For The Surviving Spouse By Year Of Birth."
https://www.ssa.gov/planners/survivors/survivorchartred.html

Once you have figured out your provisional income (also called "combined income"), you can use the following chart to figure out your Social Security taxes.[33]

Taxes on Social Security		
Provisional Income = Adjusted Gross Income + Nontaxable Interest + ½ of Social Security		
If you are ___ and your provisional income is ___, then...		Uncle Sam will tax ___ of your Social Security
Single	Married, filing jointly	
Less than $25,000	Less than $32,000	0%
$25,000 to $34,000	$32,000 to $44,000	Up to 50%
More than $34,000	More than $44,000	Up to 85%

This is one more reason it may benefit you to work with financial and tax professionals. They can look at your entire financial picture to make your overall retirement plan as tax-efficient as possible—including your Social Security benefit.

I try to help my clients stay below these thresholds. In some cases, it's not possible or practical to do this. Yet, if you position your income strategically, you'll pay less in taxes. It's plain and simple. And that means more for you, your family, your goals, and your dreams.

---

[33] Social Security Administration. "Benefits Planner: Income Taxes and Your Social Security Benefits." https://www.ssa.gov/planners/taxes.html

Working and Social Security: The Earnings Test

If you haven't reached FRA, but you started your Social Security benefits and are still working, things get a little hairy.

Because you have started Social Security payments, the Social Security Administration will pay out your benefits (at that reduced rate, of course, because you haven't reached your FRA). Yet, because you are working, the organization must also withhold from your check to add to your benefits, which you are already collecting. See how this complicates matters?

To straighten the situation, the government has what is called the earnings test. For 2020, you can earn up to $18,240 without it affecting your Social Security check. But, for every $2 you earn past that amount, the Social Security Administration will withhold $1. The earnings test loosens in the year of your FRA; if you are reaching FRA in 2020, you can earn up to $48,600 before you run into the earnings test, and the government only withholds $1 for every $3 past that amount. The month you reach FRA, you are no longer subject to any earnings withholding. For instance, if you are still working and will turn sixty-six on December 28, 2020, you would only have to worry about the earnings test until December, and then you can ignore it entirely. Keep in mind, the money the government withholds from your Social Security benefits while you are working before FRA will be tacked back onto your benefits check after FRA.[34]

As I've mentioned, some benefits come to those who wait to draw on these funds. Having the legal ability to collect these benefits doesn't mean it's the wisest course of action. Try to see how these benefits fit into the big picture. I help my clients

---

[34] Social Security Administration. "Exempt Amounts Under the Earnings Test." https://www.ssa.gov/oact/cola/rtea.html

balance their other forms of retirement income so they can best do this.

Many financial professionals say Social Security is the foundation of all retirement income. Whether or not that is true, it's always going to be there for you. Social Security is a major piece in the retirement puzzle. Understanding where this piece fits in is essential to unveil the larger picture. This chapter has explained the basics, but if you really want to get the most out of your Social Security benefits, consult an experienced financial professional.

You want to have a secure retirement. You want to leave as much as you can for your family. Maximizing the potential of your Social Security benefits unlocks effective strategies to accomplish those goals.

CHAPTER 6

401(k)s & IRAs

Have you heard? Today's retirement is not your parents' retirement. You see, back in the day, it was pretty common to work for one company for the vast majority of your career and then retire with a gold watch and a pension.

The gold watch was a symbol of the quality time you had put in at that company, but the pension was more than a symbol. Instead, it was a guarantee—as solid as your employer—that they would repay your hard work with a certain amount of income in your old age. Did you see the caveat there? Your pension's guarantee was *as solid as your employer*. The problem was, what if your employer went under?

Companies that failed couldn't pay their retired employees' pensions, leading to financial challenges for many. Beginning in 1974 with Congress' passage of the Employee Retirement Income Security Act, federal legislation and regulations aimed at protecting retirees were everywhere. One piece of legislation included a relatively obscure section of the Internal Revenue Code, added in 1978. Section 401(k), to be specific.

IRC section 401, subsection k, created tax advantages for employer-sponsored financial products, even if the main contributor was the employee him or herself. Over the years, more employers took note, beginning an age of transition away from pensions and toward 401(k) plans. A 401(k) is a retirement account with certain tax benefits and restrictions on the investments or other financial products inside of it.

Essentially, 401(k)s and their individual retirement account (IRA) counterparts are "wrappers" that provide tax benefits around assets; typically, the assets that compose IRAs and 401(k)s are mutual funds, stock and bond mixes, and money market accounts. However, IRA and 401(k) contents are becoming more diverse these days, with some companies offering different kinds of annuity options within their plans.

Where pensions are defined-*benefit* plans, 401(k)s and IRAs are defined-*contribution* plans. The one-word change outlines the basic difference. Pensions spell out what you can expect to receive from the plan but not necessarily how much money it will take to fund those benefits. With 401(k)s, an employer sets a standard for how much they will contribute (if any), and you can be certain of what you are contributing. Still, there is no outline for what you can expect to receive in return for those contributions.

Modern employment looks very different. A 2018 survey by the Bureau of Labor Statistics determined U.S. workers stayed with their employers a median of about four years. Workers ages fifty-five to sixty-four had a little more staying power and were most likely to stay with their employer for about ten years.[35] Additionally, the outlook on the benefits front is different today, too. In 1979, 38 percent of workers had pensions. But 401(k)s are rising in number, with about 55 million American workers enrolled in a plan.[36]

A far cry from a pension and gold watch, wouldn't you say?

This transition has created the need for an entirely new kind of planning. With this shift, the burden of responsibility and the burden of risk is on you, the employee. That means you have to

---

[35] Bureau of Labor Statistics. September 20,2018. "Employee Tenure Summary." https://www.bls.gov/news.release/tenure.nr0.htm

[36] Investment Company Institute. December 31, 2018. "Frequently Asked Questions about 401(k) Plan Research." https://www.ici.org/policy/retirement/plan/401k/faqs_401k

make good choices. While you can still enjoy the same basic comforts of retirement, you now need to dedicate more time, effort, and attention to making it there.

If there is anything to learn from this paradigm shift, it's that you must look out for yourself. Whether you have worked for a company for two years or twenty, you are still the one who has to look out for your own best interests. That holds doubly true when it comes to preparing for retirement. If you are one of the lucky ones who still has a pension, good for you. But for the rest of us, it is likely a 401(k)—or possibly one of its nonprofit- or government-sector counterparts, a 403(b) or 457 plan—is one of your biggest assets for retirement.

Some employers offer incentives to contribute to their company plans, like a company match. On that subject, I have one thing to say: *Do it!* Nothing in life is free, as they say, but a company match on your retirement funds is about as close to free money as it gets. If you can make the minimum to qualify for your company's match at all, go for it.

Now, it's likely, during our working years, we mostly "set and forget" our 401(k) funding. Because it is tax-advantaged, your employer is taking money from your paycheck—before taxes—and putting it into your plan for you. Maybe you got to pick a selection of investments, or maybe your company only offers one choice of investment in your 401(k). Either way, while you are gainfully employed, your most impactful decision may just be the decision to continue funding your plan in the first place. But, when you are ready to retire or move jobs, you have choices to make requiring a little more thought and care.

When you are ready to part ways with your job, you have a few options:

- Leave the money where it is
- Take the cash (and pay income taxes and perhaps a 10 percent additional federal tax if you are younger than age fifty-nine-and-one-half)

- Transfer the money to another employer plan (if the new plan allows)
- Roll the money over into a self-directed IRA

Now, these are just general options. Hopefully with the help of a financial professional, you will have to decide what's right for you. For instance, 401(k)s are typically pretty closely tied to the companies offering them, so, when changing jobs, it may not always be possible to transfer a 401(k) to another 401(k). Leaving the money where it is may also be out of the question—some companies have direct cash payout or rollover policies once someone is no longer employed.

Also, remember what we said earlier about how we change jobs more often these days? That means you likely have a 401(k) with your current company, but you may also have a string of retirement accounts trailing you from other jobs.

I worked with a man named Jim. He was self-employed but had worked for quite a number of companies over the years. When we were evaluating his assets, he told me he had five IRAs. But, as he gave me more details about his working life, I had the sneaking suspicion he had more accounts than he realized. I asked him to double-check his records to make sure he wasn't missing anything.

He came back to me and said, "Todd, you were right. I actually have nine IRAs!" Jim's experience is not unique. I meet people like this now more often than ever before.

While having more money than you realize might seem like a blessing, there's a hidden danger. If you don't know what you have, how can you make your money work for you? You can't make assets grow if you don't know they exist.

When it comes to your retirement income, it's important to be able to pull together *all* your assets, so you can examine what you have and where, and then decide what you will do with it.

Tax-Qualified, Tax-Preferred, Tax-Deferred ... Still TAXED

Financial media often cite IRAs and 401(k)s for their tax benefits. After all, with traditional plans, you put your money in, pre-tax, and it hopefully grows for years, even decades, untaxed. That's why these accounts are called "tax-qualified" or "tax-deferred" assets. They aren't *tax-free!* Rarely does Uncle Sam allow business to continue without receiving his piece of the pie, and your retirement assets are no different. If you didn't pay taxes on the front end, you will pay taxes on the money you withdraw from these accounts in retirement. Don't get me wrong: This isn't an inherently good or bad thing; it's just the way it is. It's important to understand, though, for the sake of planning ahead.

In retirement, many people assume they will be in a lower tax bracket. Are you planning to pare down your lifestyle in retirement? Perhaps you are, and perhaps you will have substantially less income in retirement. But many of my clients tell me they want to live life more or less the same as they always have. The money they would previously have spent on business attire or gas for their commute they now want to spend on hobbies and grandchildren. That's all fine, and, for many of them, it is doable, but does it put them in a lower tax bracket? Probably not.

Keep in mind, IRAs, 401(k)s, and their alternatives have a few limitations because of their special tax status. For one thing, the IRS sets limits on your contributions to these retirement accounts. If you are contributing to a 401(k) or an equivalent nonprofit or government plan, your annual contribution limit is $19,500 (as of 2020). If you are fifty or older, the IRS allows additional contributions, called "catch-up contributions," of up to $6,500 on top of the regular limit of

$19,500. For an IRA, the limit is $6,000, with a catch-up limit of an additional $1,000. [37]

Because their tax advantages come from their intended use as retirement income, withdrawing funds from these accounts before you turn fifty-nine-and-one-half can carry stiff penalties. In addition to fees your investment management company might charge, you will have to pay income tax *and* a 10 percent federal tax penalty, with few exceptions.

The fifty-nine-and-one-half rule for retirement accounts is incredibly important to remember, especially when you're young. Younger workers are often tempted to cash out an IRA from a previous employer and then are surprised to find their checks missing 20 percent of the account value to income taxes, penalty taxes, and account fees.

Many millennials I see in my practice say, while they may be socking money away in their workplace retirement plan, it is often the *only* place they are saving. This could be problematic later because of the fifty-nine-and-one-half rule; what if you have an emergency? It is important to fund your retirement, but you need to have some liquid assets handy as emergency funds. This can help you avoid breaking into your retirement accounts and incurring taxes and penalties because of the fifty-nine-and-one-half rule.

RMDs

Remember how we talked about the 401(k) or IRA being a "tax wrapper" for your funds? Well, eventually, Uncle Sam will want a bite of that candy bar. So, when you turn seventy-two, the government requires you withdraw a portion of your account, which the IRS calculates based on the size of your

---

[37] Troy Segal. Investopedia. January 17, 2020. "What Are the Roth 401(k) Contribution Limits?"
https://www.investopedia.com/ask/answers/102714/what-are-roth-401k-contibution-limits.asp

account and your estimated lifespan. This required minimum distribution, or RMD, is the government's insurance it will collect some taxes, at some point, from your earnings. Because you didn't pay taxes on the front end, you will now pay income taxes on whatever you withdraw, including your RMDs. Also, let me just remind you not to play chicken with the U.S. government; if you don't take your RMDs starting at seventy-two, you will have to write a check to the IRS for *50 percent* of the amount of your missed RMDs. With the change in law from the SECURE Act of 2019, even after you begin RMDs, you can still also continue contributing to your 401(k) or IRAs if you are still employed, which can affect the whole discussion on RMDs and possible tax considerations.

If you don't need income from your retirement accounts, RMDs can seem like more of a tax burden than an income boon. While some people prefer to reinvest their RMDs, this comes with the possibility of additional taxation: You'll pay income taxes on your RMDs and then capital gains taxes on the growth of your investments. If you are legacy minded, there are other ways to use RMDs, many of which have tax benefits.

Permanent Life Insurance

One way to turn those pesky RMDs into a legacy is through permanent life insurance. Assuming you need the death benefit coverage and can qualify for it medically, if properly structured, these products can pass on a sizeable death benefit to your beneficiaries, tax-free, as part of your general legacy plan.

ILIT

Another way to use RMDs toward your legacy is to work with an estate planning attorney to create an irrevocable life insurance trust (ILIT). This is basically a permanent life insurance policy placed within a trust. Because the trust is irrevocable, you would relinquish control of it, but, unlike with just a permanent life insurance policy, your death benefit won't count toward your taxable estate.

Annuities

Because annuities can be tax-deferred, using all or a portion of your RMDs to fund an annuity contract can be one way to further delay taxation while guaranteeing income payments (either to you or your loved ones) later (assuming you don't need the income from the RMDs during your retirement).

Qualified Charitable Distributions

If you are charity-minded, you may use your RMDs toward a charitable organization instead of using them for income. You must do this directly from your retirement account (you can't take the RMD check and *then* pay the charity) for your withdrawals to be qualified charitable distributions (QCDs), but this is one way of realizing some of the benefits of a charitable legacy during your own lifetime. You will not need to pay taxes on your QCDs, and they won't count toward your annual charitable tax deduction limit, plus you'll be able to see how the organization you are supporting uses your donations. You should consult a financial professional on how to correctly make a QCD, particularly since the SECURE Act of 2019 has implemented a few regulations on this point.[38]

Roth IRA

Since the Taxpayer Relief Act of 1997, there has been a different kind of retirement account, or "tax wrapper," available to the

---

[38] Bob Carlson. Forbes. January 28, 2020. "More Questions And Answers About The SECURE Act."
https://www.forbes.com/sites/bobcarlson/2020/01/28/more-questions-and-answers-about-the-secure-act/#113d49564869

public: the Roth. Roth IRAs and Roth 401(k)s each differ from their traditional counterparts in one big way: You pay your taxes on the front end. This means, once your post-tax money is in the Roth account, as long as you follow the rules and limitations of that account, your distributions are truly tax-free. You won't pay income tax when you take withdrawals, so, in turn, you don't have to worry about RMDs. However, Roth accounts have the same limitations as traditional 401(k)s and IRAs when it comes to withdrawing money before age fifty-nine-and-one-half, with the added stipulation that the account must have been open for at least five years in order for the accountholder to make withdrawals.

You can convert funds from a traditional IRA or 401(k) to its respective Roth counterpart. When making these conversions, there are a number of angles I like to consider with my clients.

First, when you convert funds to a Roth account, you have to pay taxes on the funds you convert. These taxes could be substantial and the future tax rate could be lower. Careful calculation is important.

Second, you have to wait five years before you can make tax-free withdrawals. This is true even if you are over fifty-nine-and-one-half. This isn't an issue for most people. But, for those nearing retirement, it could be a deal-breaker.

It is great to have an account that is tax-free and growing. But these factors could complicate matters. You have to make sure a Roth conversion makes sense for you.

Taking Charge

As mentioned earlier, the 401(k) and IRA have largely replaced pensions, but they aren't an equal trade.

Pensions are employer-funded; the money feeding into them is money that wouldn't ever show up on your pay stub. Because 401(k)s are self-funded, you must actively and consciously save. This distinction has made a difference when it comes to funding retirement. According to one NerdWallet article, the average 401(k) balance for a person age sixty to sixty-nine is $198,600, but the median likely tells the full story. The median 401(k) balance for a person age sixty to sixty-nine is $63,000. The article also cites the general suggestion to aim, by age thirty, to have saved up an amount equal to 50 percent to 100 percent of your annual salary.[39] For some thirty-year-olds, saving half an annual salary by age thirty is more than some sixty-to-sixty-nine-year-olds have saved for their entire lives.

There can be many reasons why people underfund their retirement plans, like being overwhelmed by the investment choices or taking withdrawals from IRAs when they leave an employer, but the reason at the top of the list is this: People simply aren't participating to begin with.

So, whether you use a 401(k) with an employer or an IRA alternative with a private company, separate from your workplace, the most important retirement savings decision you can make is to sock away your money somewhere in the first place.

---

[39] Arielle O'Shea. Nerd Wallet. January 24, 2019. "The Average 401(k) Balance by Age." https://www.nerdwallet.com/article/investing/the-average-401k-balance-by-age

CHAPTER 7

Annuities

In my practice, I offer my clients a variety of products—from securities to insurance—all designed to help them reach their financial goals. You may be wondering: Why single out a single product in this book?

Well, while most of my clients have a pretty good understanding of business and finance, I sometimes find those who have the impression there must be magic involved. Some people assume there is a magic finance wand we can wave to change years' worth of savings into a strategy for retirement income. But it's not as easy as a goose laying golden eggs or the Fairy Godmother turning a pumpkin into a coach!

Finances aren't magic; it takes lots of hard work and, typically, several financial products and strategies to pull together a complete retirement plan. Of all the financial products I work with, it seems people find none more mysterious than annuities. And, if I may say, even some of those who recognize the word "annuity" have a limited understanding of the product. So, in the interest of demystifying annuities, let me tell you a little about what an annuity is.

In general, insurance is a financial hedge against risk. Car owners buy auto insurance to protect their finances in case they injure someone or someone injures them. Homeowners have house insurance to protect their finances in case of a fire, flood, or another disaster. People have life insurance to protect their finances in case of untimely death. Almost juxtaposed to life insurance, people have annuities in case of a long life; annuities can give you financial protection by providing consistent and reliable income payments.

The basic premise of an annuity is you, the annuitant, pay an insurance company some amount in exchange for their contractual guarantee they will pay you income for a certain time period. How that company pays you, for how long, and how much they offer are all determined by the annuity contract you enter into with the insurance company.

How You Get Paid

There are two ways for an annuity contract to provide income: The first is through what is called annuitization, and the second is through the use of income riders. We'll get into income riders in a bit, but let's talk about annuitization. That nice, long word is, in my opinion, one reason annuities have a reputation for mystery and misinformation.

Annuitization

When someone "annuitizes" a contract, it is the point where he or she turns on the income stream. Once a contract has been annuitized, there is no going back. With annuities, if the policyholder lives longer than the insurance company planned, the insurance company is still obligated to pay him or her, even if the payments end up being way more than the contract's actual value. If, however, the policyholder dies an untimely death, depending on the contract type, the insurance company may keep anything left of the money that funded the annuity—nothing would be paid out to the contract holder's survivors. You see where that could make some people balk? Now, modern annuities rarely rely on annuitization for the income portion of the contract, and instead have so many bells and whistles that the old concept of annuitization seems outdated; but, because this is still an option, it's important to at least understand the basic concept.

Riders

Speaking of bells and whistles, let's talk about riders. Modern annuities have a lot of different options these days, many in the form of riders you can add to your contract for a fee—usually about 1 percent of the contract value per year. Each rider has its particulars, and the types of riders available will vary by the type of annuity contract purchased, but I'll just briefly outline some of these little extras:

- Lifetime income rider: Contract guarantees you an enhanced income for life
- Death benefit rider: Contract pays an enhanced death benefit to your beneficiaries even if you have annuitized
- Return of premium rider: Guarantees you (or your beneficiaries) will at least receive back the premium value of the annuity
- Long-term care rider: Provides a certain amount, sometimes as much as twice the principal value of the contract, to help pay for long-term care if the contract holder is moved to a nursing home or assisted living situation

This isn't an extensive look, and usually the riders have fancier names based on the issuing company, like "Lorem Ipsum Insurance Company Income Preferred Bonus Fixed Index Annuity rider," but I just wanted to show you what some of the general options are in layperson's terms.

Types of Annuities

Annuities break down into four basic types: immediate, variable, fixed, and fixed index.

Immediate

Immediate annuities primarily rely on annuitization to provide income—you give the insurance company a lump sum up front, and your payments begin immediately. Once you begin receiving income payments, the transaction is irreversible, and you no longer have access to your money in a lump sum. When you die, any remaining contract value is typically forfeited to the insurance company.

All other annuity contract types are "deferred" contracts, meaning you fund your policy as a lump sum or over a period of years and you give it the opportunity to grow over time—sometimes years, sometimes decades.

Variable

A variable annuity is an insurance contract as well as an investment. It's sold by insurance companies, but only through someone who is registered to sell investment products. With a variable annuity contract, the insurance company invests your premiums in subaccounts tied to the stock market. This makes it a bit different from the other annuity contract types because it is the only contract where your money is subject to losses because of market declines. Your contract value has a greater opportunity to grow, but it also stands to lose. Additionally, your contract's value will be subject to the underlying investment's fees and limitations—including capital gains taxes, management fees, etc. Once it is time for you to receive income from the contract, the insurance company will pay you a certain income, locked in at whatever your contract's value was.

Variable annuities have a place in our financial world; however, the risks are high. I generally do not recommend variable annuities. I've only seen three or four instances where a variable annuity purchase proved to be truly successful in my twenty years of business.

On top of the high risk, there are fees. And, on top of the fees, there are more fees. These fees eat away at potential gains and, ultimately, your retirement. Unless a variable annuity policy has certain riders, there will always be products that accomplish the same thing with less risk and expense.

That doesn't mean variable annuities are bad. But, when you have high risk and high fees in any financial situation, the numbers are stacked against you.

So, my advice: Be careful with variable annuities.

Fixed

A traditional fixed annuity is pretty straightforward. You purchase a contract with a guaranteed interest rate and when you are ready, the insurance company will make regular income payments to you at whatever payout rate your contract guarantees. Those payments will continue for the rest of your life and, if you choose, for the remainder of your spouse's life.

Fixed annuities don't have much in the way of upside potential, but many people like them for their guarantees, as well as for their predictability. (After all, if your Aunt May lives to be ninety-five, knowing she has a paycheck later in life can be her mental and financial safety net.) Unlike variable annuities, which are subject to market risk and might be up one year and down the next, you can easily calculate the value of your fixed annuity over your lifetime.

Fixed Index

To recap, variable annuities take on more risk to offer more possibilities to grow. Fixed annuities have less potential growth, but they protect your principal. In the last couple of decades, many insurance companies have retooled their product line to offer fixed index annuities, which are sort of midway between variable and fixed annuities on that risk/reward spectrum. Fixed index annuities offer greater growth potential than traditional fixed annuities but less than variable annuities. Like traditional fixed annuities, however, fixed index annuities are protected from downside market losses.

Fixed index annuities earn interest that is tied to the market, meaning that, instead of your contract value growing at a set interest rate like a traditional fixed annuity, it has the potential to grow within a range. Your contract's value is credited interest based on the performance of an external market index like the S&P 500 while never being invested in the market itself. You can't invest in the S&P 500 directly, but each year, your annuity has the potential to earn interest based on the chosen index's performance, subject to limits set by the company, such as caps, spreads, and participation rates. For instance, if your contract caps your interest at 5 percent, then, in a year the S&P 500 gains 3 percent, your annuity value increases 3 percent. If the S&P 500 gains 35 percent, your annuity value gets a 5 percent interest bump. But, since your money isn't actually invested in the market with a fixed index annuity, if the market nosedives (such as what happened during 2000, 2008, and 2020, anyone?) you won't see any increase in your contract value. Conversely, there will also be no decrease in your contract value—no matter how badly the market performed, as long as you follow the terms of the contract, you won't lose any of the interest you were credited in previous years.

So, what if the S&P 500 shows a market loss of 30 percent? Your contract value isn't going anywhere (unless you purchased an optional rider—this charge will still come out of your annuity value each year). For those who are more interested in protection than growth potential, fixed index annuities can be an attractive option because, when the stock market has a long period of positive performance, a fixed index annuity can enjoy conservative growth. And, during stretches where the stock market is erratic and stock values across the board take significant losses? Fixed index annuities won't lose anything due to the stock market volatility.

I make ample use of these products in my practice. People like the idea of "zero risk" and "guaranteed growth." That being said, these products are over-advertised, over-sold, and overestimated.

Not all fixed index annuity products are created equal. There are so many of these products, and all of them are different. You have to do your research. There are some great products out there, but they're a time investment. Don't expect great or rapid growth. These products are generally reliable, but it's still important not to overestimate the place they should play in your retirement plan.

Other Things to Know About Annuities

We just talked about the four kinds of annuity contracts available, but all of them have some commonalities as annuities.

For all annuities, the contractual guarantees are only as strong as the insurance company that sells the product, which makes it important to thoroughly check the credit ratings of any company whose products you are considering.

Annuities are tax-deferred, meaning you don't have to pay taxes on interest earnings each year as the contract value grows. Instead, you will pay ordinary income taxes on your withdrawals. These are meant to be long-term products, so, like other tax-deferred or tax-advantaged products, if you begin taking withdrawals from your contract before age fifty-nine-and-one-half, you may also have to pay a 10 percent federal tax penalty. Also, while annuities are generally considered illiquid, most contracts allow you to withdraw up to 10 percent of your contract value every year. Withdraw any more, however, and you could incur additional surrender penalties.

Keep in mind, your withdrawals will deplete the accumulated cash value, death benefit, and, possibly, the rider values of your contract.

Your retirement plan is a lot like a tree. A tree has a trunk and branches that continually grow, and it has a root system that stabilizes this growth. When a storm comes, a tree will stand strong because its roots have the power to support it. The tree might lose a few branches, but that's hardly an issue. Your retirement plan is the same. You have your growth products and liquid assets. Should a storm in the market or your personal life come, these assets would be the first to go. But that really won't matter if your plan is strong enough. The roots, your stabilizing assets, will keep your plan sturdy.

Annuities are a kind of product that stabilizes your plan. If everything else goes wrong, they have the power to provide for you during retirement.

Annuities aren't for everyone, but it's important to understand them before saying "yea" or "nay" on whether they fit into your plan; otherwise, you're not operating with complete information, wouldn't you agree? Regardless, you should talk to a financial professional who can help you understand annuities, help you dissect your particular financial needs, and help show you whether an annuity is appropriate for your retirement income plan.

CHAPTER 8

Estate & Legacy

In my practice, I devote a significant portion of my time to matters of estates. That doesn't mean drawing up wills or trusts or putting together powers of attorney or anything like that. After all, I'm not an estate planning attorney. But, I am a financial professional, and what part of the "estate" isn't affected by money matters?

I've included this chapter because I have seen many people do estate planning wrong. Clients, or clients' families, have come in after experiencing a death in the family and have found themselves in the middle of probate, high taxes, or a discovery of something unforeseen (often long-term care) draining the estate.

I have also seen people do estate planning right: clients or families who visit my office to talk about legacies and how to make them last and adult children who have room to grieve without an added burden of unintended costs, without stress from a family ruptured because of inadequate planning.

I'll share some of these stories here. However, I'm not going to give you specific advice, since everyone's situation is unique. I only want to give you some things to think about and to underscore the importance of planning ahead.

I regularly consult with legal professionals when advising my clients. I view it as an absolute necessity. A qualified attorney can ensure your wishes come to fruition. They will help you to walk out of life with your hard-earned estate transferring to the people you love most.

You Can't Take It With You

When it comes to legacy and estate planning, the most important thing is to *do it*. I have heard people from clients to celebrities (rap artist Snoop Dogg comes to mind) say they aren't interested in what happens to their assets when they die because they'll be dead. That's certainly one way to look at it. But I think that's a very selfish way to go about things—we all have people and causes we care about, and those who care about us. Even if the people we love don't *need* what we leave behind, they can still be fined or legally tied up in the probate process or burial costs if we don't plan for those. And that's not even considering what happens if you become incapacitated at some point while you are still alive. Having a plan in place can greatly reduce the stress of those responsibilities on your loved ones; it's just a loving thing to do.

Documents

There are a few documents that lay the groundwork of legacy planning. You've probably heard of all or most of them, but I'd like to review what they are and how people commonly use them. These are all things you should talk about with an estate planning attorney to establish your legacy.

Powers of Attorney

A power of attorney, or POA, is a document giving someone the authority to act on your behalf and in your best interests. These come in handy in situations where you cannot be present (think a vacation where you get stuck in Canada) or, for durable powers of attorney, even when you are incapacitated (think in a coma or coping with dementia).

It is important to have powers of attorney in place and to appoint someone you trust to act on your behalf in these matters. Have you ever heard of someone who was incapacitated after a car accident, whether from head trauma or being in a coma for weeks—sometimes months? Do you think their bills stopped coming due during that time? I like my phone company and my bank, but neither one is about to put a moratorium on sending me bills, particularly not for an extended or interminable period. A power of attorney would have the authority to pay your mortgage or cancel your cable while you are unable.

You can have multiple POAs and require them to act jointly.

What this looks like: Do you think two heads are better than one? One man, Chris, significantly relied on his two sons' opinions for both his business and personal matters. He appointed both sons as joint POA, requiring both their signoffs for his medical and financial matters.

You can have multiple POAs who can act independently.

What this looks like: Irene had three children with whom she routinely stayed. They lived in different areas of the country, which she thought was an advantage; one month she might be hiking out West, the next she could enjoy the newest off-Broadway production, and the next she could soak up some Southern sun. She named her three children as independently authorized POAs, so, if something happened, no matter where she was, the child closest could step in to act on her behalf.

You can have POAs who have different responsibilities.

What this looks like: Although Luke's friend Claire, a nurse, was his go-to and POA for health-related issues, financial matters usually made her nervous, so he appointed his good neighbor, Matt, as his POA in all of his financial and legal matters.

In addition to POAs, it may be helpful to have an advanced medical directive. This is a document where you have pre-decided what choices you would make about different health scenarios. An advanced medical directive can help ease the burden for your medical POA and loved ones, particularly when it comes to end-of-life care.

Wills

Perhaps the most basic document of legacy planning, a will is a legal document wherein you outline your wishes for your estate. When it comes to your estate after your death, having a will is the foundation of your legacy. Without one, your loved ones are left behind, guessing what you would have wanted, and the court will likely split your assets according to the state's defaults. Maybe that's exactly what you wanted, as far as anyone knows, right? Because even if you told your nephew he could have your car he's been driving, if it's not in writing, it still might go to the brother, sister, son, or daughter to whom you aren't speaking.

However, it may not be enough just to have a will. Even with a will, your assets will be subject to probate. Probate is what we call the state's process for determining a will's validity. A judge will go through your will to question if it conflicts with state law, if it is the most up-to-date document, if you were mentally competent at the time it was in order, etc. For some, this is a quick, easily-resolved process. For others, particularly if someone steps forward to contest the will, it may take years to settle, all the while subjecting the assets to court costs and attorney's fees.

One other undesirable piece of the probate process is that it is a public process. That means anyone can go to the courthouse, ask for copies of the case, and discover your assets. They can also see who is slated to receive what and who is disputing.

It's also important to remember beneficiary lines trump wills. So, that large life insurance policy? What if, when you bought it fifteen years ago, you wrote your ex-husband's name on the beneficiary line? Even if you stipulate otherwise in your will, the company that holds your policy will pay out to your ex-spouse. Or, how about the thousands of dollars in your IRA you dedicated to the children thirty years ago, but one of your children was killed in a car accident, leaving his wife and two toddlers behind? That IRA is going to transfer to your remaining children, with nothing for your daughter-in-law and grandchildren.

That may paint a grim portrait, but I can't underscore enough the importance of working with a skilled estate planning attorney to keep your will and beneficiary lines up to date as your life changes, for the sake of your loved ones.

Being proactive in this way can help you dodge the bullet of a gun you didn't even know was loaded.

Case in point: I met a retired couple after a class I taught on estate planning. They had been married for over thirty years, but the husband had been married once before. A point I had mentioned about checking the beneficiaries on retirement accounts caught their attention. The couple double-checked to make sure the right beneficiary was listed and found something alarming. The name listed on the husband's 401(k) was his ex-wife's. This account contained hundreds of thousands of dollars. After chatting with them for a while, the wife thanked me. She said, "I get scared thinking about what might have happened if you hadn't told us to check our accounts!"

Trusts

Another piece of legacy planning to consider is the trust.

A trust is set up through an attorney and allows a third party, or trustee, to hold your assets and determine how they will pass to your beneficiaries. Many people are skeptical of trusts because they assume trusts are only appropriate for the fabulously wealthy.

However, a simple trust may only cost $1,000 to $2,500 in attorney's fees and can avoid both the expense and publicity of probate, provide a more immediate transfer of wealth, avoid some taxes, and provide you greater control over your legacy.[40]

For instance, if you want to set aside some funds for a grandchild's college education, you can make it a requirement he or she enrolls in classes before your trust will dispense any funds. Like a will, beneficiary lines will override your trust conditions, so you must still keep insurance policies and other assets up to date.

Like any financial or legal consideration, there are many options these days beyond the simple "yes or no" question of whether to have a trust. For one thing, you will need to consider if you want your trust to be revocable (you can change the terms while you are alive) or irrevocable (can't be changed; you are no longer the "owner" of the contents). A brief note here about irrevocable trusts: Although they have significant and greater tax benefits, they are still subject to a Medicaid look-back period. This means, if you transfer your assets into an irrevocable trust in an attempt to shelter them from a Medicaid spend-down, you will be ineligible for Medicaid coverage of long-term care for five years. Yet, an irrevocable trust can avoid both probate and estate taxes, and it can even protect assets from legal judgments against you.

---

[40] Regan Rondinelli-Haberek. LegalZoom. "What is the Average Cost to Prepare a Living Trust?" https://info.legalzoom.com/average-cost-prepare-living-trust-26932.html

Another thing to remember when it comes to trusts, in general, is, even if you have set up a trust, you must remember to fund it. In my twenty years' work, I've had numerous clients come to me, assuming they have protected their assets with a trust. When we talk about taxes and other pieces of their legacy, it turns out they never retitled any assets or changed any paperwork on the assets they wanted in the trust. So, please remember, a trust is just a bunch of fancy legal papers if you haven't followed through on retitling your assets.

Taxes

Although charitable contributions, trusts, and other tax-efficient strategies can reduce your tax bill, it's unlikely your estate will be passed on entirely tax-free. Yet, when it comes to building a legacy that can last for generations, taxes can be one of the heaviest drains on the impact of your hard work.

For 2017, the federal estate exemption was $5.49 million per individual and $10.98 million for a married couple, with estates facing up to a 40 percent tax rate after that. In 2020, those limits increased to $11.58 million for individuals and $23.16 million for married couples, with the 40 percent top level gift and estate tax remaining the same. Currently, the new estate limits are set to increase with inflation until Jan. 1, 2026, when they will "sunset" back to the inflation-adjusted 2017 limits.[41,42] And that's not taking into account the various state regulations and taxes regarding estate and inheritance transfers.

---

[41] Ashlea Ebeling. Forbes. December 21, 2018. "Final Tax Bill Includes Huge Estate Tax Win for the Rich: The $22.4 Million Exemption."
https://www.forbes.com/sites/ashleaebeling/2017/12/21/final-tax-bill-includes-huge-estate-tax-win-for-the-rich-the-22-4-million-exemption/
[42] Ashlea Ebeling. Forbes. November 6, 2019. "IRS Announces Higher Estate And Gift Tax Limits For 2020."
https://www.forbes.com/sites/ashleaebeling/2019/11/06/irs-announces-higher-estate-and-gift-tax-limits-for-2020/#18b9e5652efb

One "frequent flyer" on the tax concern list: retirement accounts.

Your IRA or 401(k) can be a source of tax issues when you pass away. For one thing, taking funds from a sizeable account can trigger a large tax bill. However, if you leave the assets in the account, there are still required minimum distributions (RMDs), which will take effect even after you die. If you pass the account to your spouse, he or she can keep taking your RMDs as is, or your spouse can retitle the account in his or her name and receive RMDs based on his or her life expectancy. Remember, if you don't take your RMDs, the IRS will take up to 50 percent of whatever your required distribution was, plus you will still have to pay income taxes whenever you withdraw that money. Thanks to rules enacted in 2020, anyone who inherits your IRA, with few exceptions (your spouse, a beneficiary less than ten years younger, or a disabled adult child, to name a few), will need to empty the account within ten years of your death.

Also—and this is a pretty big also—check with an attorney if you are considering putting your IRA or 401(k) in a trust. An improperly titled beneficiary form for the IRA could mean the difference of thousands of dollars in taxes. This is just one more reason to work with a financial professional, one who can strategically partner with an estate planning attorney to diligently check your decisions.

You know the saying: 'Nothing is certain in this world except death and taxes.' While those two things seem so inescapable, we can take action at least to limit the latter's effect on our lives and the lives of our families.

I've seen how careful and thorough estate planning gives my clients a sense of accomplishment and a sense of peace. The sadness your family will endure when you pass is enough of a burden. They will never have to face the challenges that come with inheriting a mismanaged estate if you are proactive.

Think about this. Even in death, you can help your family with future challenges if you plan properly now.

CHAPTER 9

Women-Specific Concerns

I help men, women, and families from all walks of life on their journey to and through retirement. Yet, I want to address the female demographic specifically. Why? To be perfectly blunt, women are more likely to deal with poverty than men when they reach retirement. One report notes nearly two-thirds of the 7.1 million older adults living in poverty in the United States are women.[43]

The topics, products, and strategies I cover elsewhere in this book are meant to help address retirement concerns for men *and* women, but those kinds of statistics are a reminder that much of traditional planning is geared toward men. Male careers, male lifespans, male health care. The bottom line is women's career paths often look much different than men's, so why would their retirement planning look the same?

Women, on average, live longer than men. This means a wife will likely outlive her husband. After he passes away, she is solely responsible for her own financial situation. If she was unfamiliar with her husband's retirement plan or financial

---

[43] Liz Seggert. Association of Health Care Journalists. January 8, 2019. "New Report Paints a Grim Picture of Older Women in Poverty." https://healthjournalism.org/blog/2019/01/new-report-paints-a-grim-picture-of-older-women-in-poverty/

standing, where would she be? Husbands, remember your wife may have to live much of her retirement without you.

It's important to find solutions to the problems afflicting retired women. I feel strongly that husbands should involve their wives in the entire retirement planning process, the finances, the goals—everything. Then they, too, become a part of the process.

Be Informed

It's a familiar scene in many financial offices across the country: A woman comes into an appointment carrying a sack full of unopened envelopes. Often through tears, she sits across the desk from a financial professional and apologizes her way through a conversation about what financial products she owns and where her income is coming from. She is recently widowed and was sure her spouse was taking care of the finances, but now she doesn't know where all their assets are kept, and her confidence in her financial outlook has wavered after walking through funeral expenses and realizing she's down to one income.

Often, she may be financially "okay." Yet, the uncertainty can be wearying, particularly when the family is already reeling from a loss. While this scenario sometimes plays out with men, in my experience, it's more likely to be a woman in that chair across from my desk, probably, in part, because of Western traditions about money management being "a guy thing." It doesn't have to be this way. This all-too-common scenario can be wiped away with just a little preparation.

Talk to Your Spouse/ Work with a Financial Professional

While there are many factors affecting women's financial preparation for and situation in retirement, I cannot emphasize enough that the decision to be informed, to be a part of the conversation, and to be aware of what is going on with your finances is absolutely paramount to a confident retirement. With all the couples I've seen, there is almost always an "alpha" when it comes to finances. It isn't always men—for many of my coupled clients, the wife is the alpha who keeps the books and budgets and knows where all of the family's assets are, down to the penny—yet, statistically, among baby boomers, it is usually a man who runs the books. But, as time goes on, it looks like the ratio of male to female financial alphas is evening out. According to a Gallup study, women are equally as likely to take the lead on finances as men, with 37 percent of U.S. households showing women primarily paying the bills. Half of households also say decisions about savings and investments are shared equally.[44] Whether that's the way your household works or not, there isn't anything wrong with who does what.

The breakdown happens when there is a lack of communication, when no one other than the financial alpha knows how much the family has and where. In the end, it doesn't matter who handles the money; it's about all parties being informed of what's going on financially.

There are a lot of ways to open up the conversation about money. One woman started a conversation with her husband, the financial alpha, by sitting down and saying, "Teach me how to be a widow." Perhaps that sounds grim, but it was to the point, and it spurred what she said was a very fruitful conversation. Couples sometimes have their first real

---

[44] Megan Brenan. Gallup. January 29, 2020. "Women Still Handle Main Household Tasks in U.S.." https://news.gallup.com/poll/283979/women-handle-main-household-tasks.aspx

conversation about money, assets, and their retirement plans in our office. The important thing about having these conversations isn't where, it's when . . . and the best "when" is as soon as possible.

Spouse-Specific Options

One area where it might be especially important to be on the same page between spouses is when it comes to financial products or services that have spousal options. A few that come to mind are pensions and Social Security, although life insurance and annuity policies also have the potential to affect both spouses.

With pensions, taking the worker's life-only option is somewhat attractive—after all, the monthly payment is bigger. However, you and your spouse should discuss your options. When we're talking about both of you, as opposed to just one lifespan, there is an increased likelihood at least one of you will live a long, long time. This means the monthly payout will be less, but it also ensures that, no matter which spouse outlives the other, no one will have to suffer the loss of a needed pension paycheck in his or her later retirement years.

While we covered Social Security options in a different chapter, I think some of the spousal information bears repeating. Particularly, if you worked exclusively inside the home for a significant number of years, you may want to talk about taking your Social Security benefits based on your spouse's work history. After all, Social Security is based on your thirty-five highest-earning years.

Things to keep in mind about Social Security spousal benefits:[45]

---

[45] Social Security Administration. "Retirement Planner: Benefits For You As A Spouse." https://www.ssa.gov/planners/retire/applying6.html

- Your benefit will be calculated as a percentage (up to 50 percent) of your spouse's earned monthly benefit at his or her full retirement age, or FRA.
- For you to begin receiving a spousal benefit, your spouse must have already filed for his or her own benefits and you must be at least sixty-two.
- You can qualify for a full half of your spouse's benefits if you wait until you reach FRA to file.
- Beginning your benefits earlier than your FRA will reduce your monthly check, but waiting to file until after FRA will not increase your benefits.

For divorcees:[46]
- You may qualify to withdraw an ex-spousal benefit if . . .
    a. You were married for a decade or more
    b. *and* you are at least sixty-two
    c. *and* you have been divorced for at least two years
    d. *and* you are currently unmarried
    e. *and* your ex-spouse is sixty-two (qualifies to begin taking Social Security)

- Your ex-spouse does not need to have filed for you to file on his or her benefit.
- Similar to spousal benefits, you can qualify for up to half of your ex-spouse's benefits if you wait to file until your FRA.
- If your ex-spouse dies, you may file to receive a widow/widower benefit on his or her Social Security record as long as you are at least age sixty and fulfill all the other requirements on the preceding alphabetized list.
    a. This will not affect the benefits of your ex-spouse's current spouse

---

[46] Social Security Administration. "Retirement Planner: If You Are Divorced." https://www.ssa.gov/planners/retire/divspouse.html

For widow's (or widower's, for that matter) benefits:[47]
- You may qualify to receive as much as your deceased spouse would have received if . . .
    a. You were married for at least nine months before his or her death
    b. *or* you would qualify for a divorced spousal benefit
    c. *and* you are at least sixty
    d. *and* you did not/have not remarried before age sixty

- You may earn delayed credits on your spouse's benefit *if* your spouse hadn't already filed for benefits when he or she died.
- Other rules may apply to you if you are disabled or are caring for a deceased spouse's dependent or disabled child.

Longevity

On average, women live longer than men. Most stats put average female longevity at about two years more than men's. But averages are tricky things. I think perhaps a more telling statistic is the fact that, according to the most recent U.S. Census data available, more than 80 percent of U.S. centenarians, those over 100, are women. That means the vast majority of the eldest elderly are women.[48]

---

[47] Social Security Administration. "Survivors Planner: If You Are The Worker's Widow Or Widower."
https://www.ssa.gov/planners/survivors/ifyou.html#h2

[48] U.S. Census Bureau. December 10, 2012. "2010 Census Report Shows More Than 80 Percent of Centenarians are Women."
https://www.census.gov/newsroom/releases/archives/2010_census/cb12-239.html

On one hand, this is a Rosie the Riveter moment. How fabulous are women? On the other hand, this reveals longstanding financial ramifications.

As was mentioned in a preceding chapter, these extra years of life are not always healthy years of life. I've personally seen many women face years of health issues that prove very expensive. Many of them endure these difficulties long after their husbands have passed away. These real situations should prompt couples to prepare for any scenario.

As usual, these problems can be overcome with the right planning. Approaching retirement with insight and a realistic perspective can protect women from difficult situations.

Simply Needing More Money in Retirement

Living longer in retirement means needing more money, period. Barring a huge lottery win or some crazy stock market action, the date you retire is likely the point at which you have the most money you will ever have. Not to put too grim a spin on it, but the problem with longevity is, the further you get away from that date, the further your dollars have to stretch. If you planned to live to a nice eighty-something but live to a nice one-hundred-something, that is *two decades* you will need to account for, monetarily.

To put this in perspective, let's say you like to drink coffee as an everyday splurge. Not accounting for inflation or leap years, a $2.50 cup-a-day habit is $18,250 over a two-decade span. Now, think of all the things you like to do that cost money. Add those up for twenty years of unanticipated costs. I think you'll see what I mean.

More Health Care Needs

In addition to the cost of living for a longer lifespan is the fact aging, plain and simple, means more health care, and more health care means more money. Women are survivors. They suffer from the morbidity-mortality paradox, which states women suffer more non-fatal illnesses throughout their lifetime than men, who experience fewer illnesses but higher mortality. Men experience less sickness in general, but they are more susceptible to death when they do experience illness.[49] So, survival is on the side of the woman. However, surviving things, like cancer, also means more checkups later in life.

Widowhood

Not only do women typically live longer than their same-age male counterparts, they also have the tendency to marry men older than themselves. The numbers bear this out: Women are four times more likely to outlive their spouses than men.[50] In addition, 50 percent of women will become widowed by age sixty-five—and many may live at least another fifteen years or more on their own.[51]

I don't say this to scare people; rather, I think it's fundamentally important to prepare my female clients for something that may be a startling, *but very likely,* scenario. At some point, most women will have to handle their financial situations on their own. A little preparation can go a long way,

---

[49] Melinda Martin-Khan. Medical Xpress. June 10, 2019. "Why Do Women Live Longer Than Men?" https://medicalxpress.com/news/2019-06-women-longer-men.html

[50] Women's Institute For A Secure Retirement. 2019. "Widowhood: Why Women need to Talk About This Issue." https://www.wiserwomen.org/resources/widowhood-fact-sheets/widowhood-why-women-need-to-talk-about-this-issue/

[51] Ibid.

and having a basic understanding of your household finances and the "who, what, where, and how much" of your family's assets is incredibly useful—it can prevent a tragic situation from being more traumatic.[52]

As if to underscore the point the financial services industry often underserves women in these situations, consider this statistic: 70 percent of widows fire their financial advisors after their spouses die.[53] In my opinion, this is because many financial professionals tend to alienate women, even when their spouses are alive. I've heard several stories of women who sat through meeting after meeting without their financial professional ever addressing a single question to them.

In our firm, when we work with couples, we work hard to make sure our retirement income strategies work for *both* people. No matter who is the financial alpha, it's important for everyone who is affected by a retirement plan to understand it.

Taxes

One of the often-unexpected aspects of widowhood is the tax bill. Many women continue similar lifestyles to the ones they shared with their spouses. This, in turn, means continuing to have a similar need for income. However, after the death of a spouse, their taxes will be calculated based on a single filer's income table, which is much less forgiving than the couple's tax rates. With proper planning, your financial professional and tax advisor may be able to help you take the sting out of your new tax status.

---

[52] Lifetime Financial Growth. June 01, 2019. "Why Are We Unprepared for Widowhood?" https://www.lifetimefinancialgrowth.com/blog/why-are-we-unprepared-for-widowhood
[53] Mercer Partners Wealth Management. September 30, 2019. "Transitions." https://www.mercerpartnerswealth.com/p/transitions

Caregiving

Of the 44 million caregivers providing unpaid, informal care for older adults, the majority are women. Most women who provide caregiving services are still in the workforce. Yet, on average, female caregivers lose around $324,044 total in wages. This doesn't even account for Social Security benefit losses or the losses of health care benefits and retirement savings.[54] This also doesn't account for maternity care, mothers who homeschool, or women who leave the workforce to care for their children in any way.

I don't repeat these statistics to scare you. Estimates typically place the monetary value of unofficial caregiving services across the United States at around $150 billion or more. Yet, I think the emotional value of the care many women provide their elderly relatives or neighbors cannot be quantified. So, to be clear, this shouldn't be taken as a "why not to provide caregiving" spiel. Instead, it should be seen as a call for "why to *prepare* for caregiving" or "how to lessen the financial and emotional burden of caregiving."

Funding Your Own Retirement

For these reasons, women need to be prepared to fund more of their own retirements. There are several savings options and products, including the spousal 401(k). Unlike a traditional 401(k), where you contribute money to a plan with your employer, a spousal 401(k) is something your spouse sets up on your behalf, so he or she can contribute a portion of the paycheck to your retirement funds. This is something to

---

[54] Where You Live Matters. November 5, 2019. "The High Costs of Caring for a Loved One." https://www.whereyoulivematters.org/the-high-costs-of-caring-for-a-loved-one/

consider, particularly for families where one spouse has dropped out of the workforce to care for a relative.

Also, if you find yourself in a caregiving role, talk to your employer's human resources department. Some companies have paid leave, special circumstance, or sick leave options you could qualify for, making it easier to cope and helping you stay in the workforce longer.

Saving Money

Women need more money to fund their retirements, period. But this doesn't have to be a significant burden—most of the time, women are better at saving, investing, and paying down debt.[55] This gives me reason to believe, as women get more involved in their finances, families will continue to be better-prepared for retirement, both *his* and *hers*.

---

55 Dori Zinn. Debt.com. December 18, 2018. "Women are Better Than Men at Money Management." https://www.debt.com/news/budgeting-saving/handling-money-women-better-money-management/

CHAPTER 8

Finding a Financial Professional

I got into the financial services industry almost by accident. Before, I didn't know what estate plans were. I didn't know what financial plans were. But I'm glad I learned.

I probably sound sappy saying this, but I count getting into this industry as a blessing. It's an industry where I can help a lot of people, and I love that. I've had the chance to make a good living as a financial advisor, but my greatest reward is helping people lead a fulfilling life.

Financial services have changed over the years. Products have changed. People's attitudes have changed. But the goal is the same: Help people manage their money wisely.

I don't put a lot of stock in titles, education, or certifications. Those things don't make someone a good advisor. An advisor could have all the credentials in the world but be dishonest and cheat you. Good people make the best advisors. They are honest, and they will tell you when they don't know about a specific product, tax law, or legal matter.

Still, you have to know what you're talking about to give good advice. So, to give a brief list of my credentials: I am a certified estate planner, a certified retirement financial advisor, a certified financial educator, and a certified financial fiduciary.

People ask me all the time, "Do I really need a financial advisor?"

It's a good question. I've met some very successful people who have done all their own financial planning. I've actually had people in my conference room whom I've told, "You don't need me; you're doing a great job!" People are taken aback by that statement. They don't expect it coming from the guy who makes a living planning other people's finances.

My profession is similar to every other profession. You could do your financial planning by yourself, just like you could do work on your car by yourself, or wire lights in your house by yourself. It is possible. But, to do so, you would need a full understanding of our financial system. The time it would take to gain and maintain that knowledge might not be worth your while. That's a decision you need to make.

There have been significant changes in the world of technology and communication over the last few decades. The internet, smartphones, and social media have changed the world as we know it. The latest news is always at our fingertips. Online banking and online shopping have significantly changed monetary transactions. These kinds of things add convenience to our lives, but they add complexity to the world of finance.

Deciphering the endless amount of information we are served is a challenge. Inaccurate or impractical information on financial matters can ruin your retirement plans. After considering these factors, I feel it's more important to have a financial advisor now than ever before.

Making the Choice

If you decide to look for a financial professional, what should you look for? You want to know who you're dealing with, so ask lots of questions.

Ask questions about their business and qualifications. Do they have a sales quota? Are they a registered investment advisor, or just insurance licensed?

Ask about their fees. What are they? Are they fixed or commission-based? What will you get for the money you pay? (I'll come back to compensation in just a moment.)

Ask about how they communicate with clients. By call? Text? Emails? How often do they communicate with clients?

Ask about their investment philosophies. Are they fine with making risky investments? Or do they err on the side of caution?

The more you ask, the more you know.

Keep an eye out for red flags. If an advisor doesn't give you straight answers to your questions, that's a bad sign. If he or she says or does anything that makes you feel uncomfortable, go with your gut—it won't usually fail you.

Forming a relationship with a financial advisor is similar to starting a romantic relationship in at least one respect: If it doesn't feel right, don't go for it. Watch out for the warning signs.

Now, to expound on the matter of monetary compensation. Number one: Good things aren't cheap, and cheap things aren't good. Yet, some financial advisors charge astronomical rates for services that are less than stellar. The key here is to get the most out of what you pay for.

There are basically two types of compensation. There's money management compensation, and then there's commissionable compensation. Money management compensation is more of a flat rate. Commissionable compensation is usually more complicated. It involves terms of payment and fees that vary from advisor to advisor.

Every financial advisor charges fees differently. So, again, ask questions. And, if they don't give you answers about money matters, move on.

Retirement is something people look forward to for their entire life. Life goes by fast. Too fast. Before you know it, you're nearing retirement age.

As you plan, it's important to ask yourself, "What do I want to do during retirement? What do I hope to accomplish? How can I prepare now?" The sooner you start preparing, the better your retirement will be. If you start late, don't fret. Your retirement won't be miserable. But, you can't waste any time getting started with a plan.

No matter what, whether your retirement is near or far, you can make it there with confidence if you plan diligently. Be proactive, not reactive. Keep your eye on the prize. You'll be there before you know it!

Acknowledgments

A special thank you to people that have made this book possible...

My grandparents, Ed and Alma Sauder. They showed me how to stay grounded and focus on what matters in life, such as family.

My parents, Judy and Adrian Pelechaty. They have shown me unconditional love and support in the good and bad times in my life.

My children, Liam and Megan Elliott. They are definitely teaching me patience and at the same time, making me a proud dad.

Lastly, I wish to thank my better half, Cynthia Smith. She has made me believe that anything is possible with the right woman by your side.

TODD ELLIOTT
About the Author

Todd Elliott and Elliott Financial Group

As the founder of Elliott Financial Group, Todd has been helping people build more secure financial futures for almost two decades. Through his unique client programs, industry experience, and constant drive to create tailored financial strategies, Todd has shown thousands of people how to protect and preserve their assets, increase their retirement income, and reduce their taxes.

Todd's understanding of retirees and their needs has been enhanced through the years by getting to know each individual client and what is important to them. Todd's business and personal life reflect his core belief that success comes from the five Fs: faith, family, finances, fitness, and fun.

www.ingramcontent.com/pod-product-compliance
Lightning Source LLC
Chambersburg PA
CBHW070652220526
45466CB00001B/407